Written for mentors, teachers and counselors to pass onto their charges, FACES is a cautionary piece for young people facing life's most challenging choices. It combines the story of the author's journey with a group of women convicted of capital crimes and serving life sentences in a Maryland maximum–security prison with vital information regarding our judicial and penal systems.

The book introduces the women—who they were before the worst day of their lives and who they are now. It describes the details of prison life and the difficulties returning citizens face upon release. It chronicles interviews with the many judicial experts and activists she has met along the way and their efforts to humanize our prisons, change archaic laws, help troubled young people find a path to a constructive life, and assist survivors as they work to reclaim their lives.

In plain non–legalese language, it fosters awareness of egregious laws that can result in a life behind bars. It warns young women of temptations that can lead to a life of drug addiction, prostitution, and victimhood in sex–based human trafficking. Finally, FACES offers advice from the women and a brief introduction to Restorative Justice, a new/old concept that encourages communication as a way to restrain violence.

FACES

Imprisoned Women and Their Struggle with the Criminal Justice System

by

Betty May

Ebook Cover Design by www.ebooklaunch.com
Formatting by Anessa Books

ISBN: 1505396263
ISBN-13:9781505396263

TABLE OF CONTENTS

DEDICATION

This book is dedicated to the Women of I-WISH.
May the future provide your second chance.

and

To my beloved Jerry
Nothing is forever,
Always is a lie.
I can only love you
*Till the day I die.**

*From the song "Take My Love"
From the film "The Glass Slipper" (1955)
Lyrics: Helen Deutsch
Music: Bronislau Kaper

ACKNOWLEDGEMENTS

THANK YOU

- To the Women of I-WISH (Incarcerated Women Inside Seeking to/for Help). Your courage and strength astound me.
- To Mary Pat Donelan for introducing me to I-WISH and to Susan Eberhard for her gentle grace.
- To Warden Brenda Shell-Eleazer for allowing the women of I-WISH to have their voices heard.
- To my wonderful critique group: Penny March, Naomi Milliner, Cecily Nabors, Lesley Moore Vossen, and honorary members Sarah Maury Swan and Diana Belchase. I am lucky to have you in my life and in my writing.
- To everyone who agreed to be interviewed for FACES. Your input was vital to the book.
- To my children: Earl, Paul, Greg, Julie, and Chris: Your love and support have gotten me through the dark days. I know you miss your dad as much as I do.
- To Kathryn Johnson: Your suggestions were wonderful. They strengthened the narrative and brought the women alive.
- To the staff of The Shalem Institute: Your loving support will always be remembered.
- To my readers: Lily Tsao, Jennifer Bell, and John Kearney. Your comments and advice were invaluable.
- To the cast of the Kennedy Center production. It was an honor to work with you.
- To Meredith Bond, formatter extraordinaire. Thank you for your patience.
- To Herbrette and Norman Richardson and Florence Simpson. You are always there.
- To Maria Spencer. A wonderful friend.

CHAPTER ONE:
How It Started

June 12, 2008

Day One of an Unexpected Journey with Unexpected Friends

At the end of a mile–long, tree–lined road, the maximum–security prison looms into view. Double rows of thick chain–link fencing, twelve to fifteen feet high, line the perimeter, topped by mounds of coiled razor wire. On the ground, inside and outside the fences, more rows of the spiked spirals tumble together in threatening heaps. Forty–foot white guard towers stand at each corner of the complex. The darkened windows at the top of the towers obscure any view of the people inside, but I catch a few glints of light. Clusters of ugly, squat, red brick buildings with narrow, vertical slit windows march into the distance.

It is 6:45 P.M.; I am here for a 7 P.M. meeting.

I detach the car key from my key ring, slip my driver's license from my wallet, grab some paper supplies, and leave everything else in the car. The rules for visitors are strict: no pocketbooks, no briefcases, no wallets, no money, no underwire bras, and no cell phones. I later learn cell phones are the biggest piece of contraband smuggled into a prison besides drugs, and the most dangerous. There have been incidences—mostly in men's prisons—wherein cell phones have been used to coordinate attacks on correctional officers, start uprisings, intimidate witnesses, and oversee gang activity inside and outside the institution. Smuggling a cell phone into a prison can result in a $10,000 fine and a year in jail.

It is a visiting night; the lobby of the gatehouse is crowded with the inmates' friends and loved ones waiting for the officers to call their names. There are several small children and two infants. I wonder if the toddlers are even aware of their surroundings.

I am allowed to take in one small notebook and two pencils. The items go through an x–ray machine and are then thoroughly examined. Remove shoes. Remove all jewelry: watch, bracelet, and necklace. Deposit everything into a little plastic basket along with my car key and driver's license. The gentlemen have to remove their belts as well; they stand around the lobby holding their pants up.

A uniformed officer waves me through the metal detector. Any metal detected is suspect—the reason for the ban against underwire bras. The alarm goes off. I jump. Then freeze. It is my late husband's wedding ring; I wear it on a chain under my shirt. I forgot about it and it triggered the alarm. I slip the chain over my head and add it to the basket. When I succeed in getting through the detector, a female officer tells me to raise my arms and proceeds with a quick pat down. She slides her hands over my shoulders and arms, under my breasts, and up and down my legs.

I retrieve my belongings, redress, turn my driver's license over to yet another officer, and receive in return a visitor's badge to clip onto my shirt. A big red "V" for "Visitor" differentiates it from the prisoners' badges, which sport a big red "I" for "Inmate."

Finally time to go in. The two people who had invited me lead the way. We wait for the first door to clang aside electronically. (They are called "sliders" and, yes, they really do clang, just as they do in movies.) Enter a tiny anteroom. Wait for the next slider to clang aside. Walk outside. Wait for another slider to clang open. Cross a courtyard enclosed by a twelve–foot chain–link fence topped by the ever–present whorls of razor wire. More wire stacks lie in a heap outside the fence and dribble down a rocky strip that leads to the road and the outside world.

Wait for the first courtyard slider to clang shut. Wait for the opposite courtyard slider to clang aside. Take the sidewalk around to one of the squat red brick buildings. Bars on all the windows. Wait for the inside slider to clang aside. Sign in. Again. Wait for another inside slider to clang aside. Go through that squat red brick building to another squat red brick building. Wait for the slider to the entrance hall to clang aside. Report to an officer and wait for the door to the offices and meeting rooms to click open. Find the right room and there they are: my future stars.

It is 7:35 P.M. I am thirty–five minutes late.
****

It began in May of 2008 with an unusual phone call:

Caller: Is this Betty May?

Me: Yes.

Caller: And you are the director and you write plays?

Me: Yes.

Caller: Could you write a comedy about life in prison?

No, it wasn't a prank. The caller was Mary Pat Donelan, founder and sponsor of I–WISH (Incarcerated Women Inside Seeking to/for Help), a group of women serving natural life sentences in a Maryland maximum–security prison. She runs the bimonthly meetings along with her co–sponsor, Susan Eberhard.

The women of I–WISH wanted to be heard and seen, Mary Pat told me. They feel invisible to the outside world—a perception grounded in reality: many of them have "victim impact" clauses in their sentences forbidding any public display of their faces. They wanted to contribute to society in any way possible from behind the walls of a maximum–security prison. And they wanted to show the world they are deserving of a second chance. They decided to launch a reach—out program for at—risk youth. Perhaps the lessons they learned from their tortured pasts could be passed on to the people who needed to hear them.

Six months earlier, they had written and presented a play designed to warn teenagers of the consequences of bad choices. It went over well with the population (a euphemism for inmates), but bombed when presented to their target audience. They concluded the teens didn't like it because it wasn't funny. That's where I came in.

After Mary Pat's call I didn't think much about "a comedy about life in prison." The meeting was a month away—the long lead—time necessary because prison officials had to run a background check on me to make sure I was on the right side of the walls. I was directing other shows and working on my novels. I am also a clown, and the end of the school year is a busy time: the usual birthday parties plus school fairs, family reunions, community events, and businesses celebrating the onset of the slow summer months with company picnics. And I was getting ready for my job as head coach at my son's summer circus camp in Greenbelt, Maryland, a fun, if exhausting, job.

People often ask if I was afraid going into a prison with "a bunch of murderers," but my late husband, Gerald (Jerry) G. May, was a psychiatrist and worked at Patuxent Institution in Maryland for several years. The "murderers" were the inmates from whom he had the least to fear. Serial killers aside (the majority of whom are men), most are people who, for one reason or another, didn't like somebody. The women had no reason to dislike me—at least not at first.

More on that later.

So, no, I felt no fear. At this point, volunteer or not, it was just another theatrical gig. If they wanted a comedy about life in prison, I would write a comedy about life in prison. No sweat. Talk to the women; get some amusing anecdotes; rewatch that wonderful 1999 movie, *Life*, starring Eddie Murphy and Martin Lawrence; invent a few scenarios… Piece of cake.

****

There were about twenty–five women at that first meeting, seated at two long tables pushed end to end. The tables filled the small room. Gray plastic chairs—some of them linked together—and beige walls decorated the space. They were all dressed in gray cotton prison–issue outfits. Because it was summer, most were wearing knee–length shorts. The gray t–shirts had three–inch white DOC (Department of Corrections) letters on the back, since changed to DPSCS (Department of Public Safety and Correctional Services). The gray shorts had three–inch white DOC letters down the length of the left pant leg. Every hairstyle possible, from bald, to braids, to dreadlocks, to cornrows, to careless or perfectly coiffed long strands. Most were thirty–five to, perhaps, seventy, but some were in their late teens and early twenties. I was surprised to see such young women in a group of lifers.

Mary Pat introduced me and said they had business to conduct before we did anything else. Much of the conversation centered on speakers for their upcoming meetings: professionals involved in the judicial system in one way or another; experts in self–improvement fields; and instructors on various topics such as poetry, meditation, and Reiki.

Some of the women stole quick glances at me. I smiled and nodded. They gave me quick ten–percent grins and looked back down at the table. A lot of them sat hunched over, as if embarrassed by the presence of an "outsider."

When it came my turn, I asked them to tell me more about what they wanted to accomplish with their play.

A large African American woman spoke first.

"We want to talk to kids in trouble," she said. "We want to help them—maybe keep them from ending up like us." She waved one hand at the women seated around the beige tables. "We wrote a play. Everybody here in the prison loved it. But when we did it for the kids they were bored. Turned off. Rolled their eyes. Wiggled around in their chairs. Couldn't wait to get out. Left without even talking to us."

"Why do you think that was?" I asked.

She shrugged her shoulders. "Don't know."

An older woman at the far end of the table spoke up. A heavy accent I later learned was Phillippine made it difficult to fully understand her words, but I got the gist.

"It wasn't funny," she said. "Kids want funny."

She tucked a strand of gray hair behind her ear and looked me straight in the face, her faded blue eyes staring into mine. "Can you write a funny play about us? Tell them about bad choices we made? Warn them?"

She was so earnest, and her concern for these unknown troubled kids was real.

I didn't know what to say. How could I write a "funny" play about people who led such miserable lives? Eddie Murphy aside, what could be funny about a *real* lifetime sentence?

I asked them to tell me about their former lives and their lives in prison. As they realized I was interested in what they had to say, they opened up a little, although the hunched backs remained and the furtive looks continued. I began to understand what I was seeing was shame and a fear of still more judgment.

"We did dumb things," a young black woman said. "Stupid things. And now we're here."

"We see kids coming in here every day," a fortyish woman who looked like a white suburban soccer mom said. "Kids just like us. We know what goes on in their homes. It's what went on in our homes that nobody talked about. We'd tell people and they wouldn't believe us."

Around the table, a few white heads bobbed in agreement. The younger black women didn't look impressed.

"That's only some of them," one said. She looked like she was still in her teens "Most of them are from the city. Went to the same damn schools we went to. Stupid kids walking around trying to look tough but scared as hell. They think being in jail is cool. We want to tell them different—what really goes down in here."

A woman somewhere between forty and sixty—her shaved head made it difficult to tell her age—had written another play.

"It's about these three inmates. They tell all about what happened to them when they were kids. How their mom's boyfriends beat the shit out of them. Then they tell what they did—how they robbed some old lady at a bus stop and she dropped dead."

She read the play out loud. It was brutal and intense—a little too intense, some of us felt, for kids. Others didn't agree. They believed it was what some kids face and should be presented.

"It is what it is," an older white woman said. "We have to tell it the way it is."

The discussion went on for quite a while without a resolution, except that the reality should be presented in a way palatable for young people.

The conversation kind of petered out, so I launched into a brief lecture on Constantin Stanislavski, the patron saint of acting.[1] I explained the basis of Method Acting: physical action to evoke emotional response. The women were willing to give it a try and we had some fun with Stanislavski's *Score of Actions*: What do you *do* when you are happy? What do you *do* when you are sad? They participated, but I caught a couple of people yawning.

I heard a whispered comment: "What's she talking about?"

Okay. Maybe it was a little early for Stanislavski.

I switched to theater games and the room exploded. They loved the exercises and everyone joined in. Purists in the theater world would not have liked it—lots of showing off and going for the laugh—but we sure had fun. I completely forgot I was in a maximum-security prison. I think, for a

---

[1] Constantin Stanislavski, 1863–1938, was a Russian actor and director. He revolutionized the art of acting.

moment or two, maybe they did, too. I don't remember the exact words, but it went something like this:

"My name is Baby Doll Susie," a three–hundred–pound woman squeaked. "And I just can't stop wetting my pants."

She got up from the table and sat on another large woman's lap. "Can you help me G.I. Joe?"

"Get off of me!" the recipient said in a deep macho voice. "You're getting my pretty uniform all wet." G.I. Joe shoved Baby Doll Susie away and Susie landed on the floor.

"I hurt my bum–bum," she sobbed.

They got into the games so quickly I decided to try some group improvisation. I clapped my hands. "All right, children. It's your first day of kindergarten. Gather 'round." I waved them into a circle.

It took them all of three seconds to get into the act.

A twenty–something black woman raised her hand. "Teacher?"

I smiled a benign kindergarten teacher smile. "Yes, Sally?"

"Johnny showed me his wee–wee."

The woman next to her jumped right in. "Did not."

"Did, too!"

"Did not!"

"Did, too! And it was this big." She held her forefinger and thumb an inch apart.

By this time we were all doubled over with laughter. But they weren't finished.

A tall woman with a long gray ponytail grabbed a piece of paper and a pencil and made a drawing of a spider. She showed it to everyone, and then shoved it down the back of another woman's shirt. Appropriate shrieks followed, along with deep, heartfelt wailing. I laughed so hard my stomach hurt.

An officer, alarmed by the noise, stepped into the room. The fluorescent light glinted off the metal buttons on her uniform.

"Everything all right in here?"

One of the younger inmates waved her off. "We're fine, Miss Dade. No problem."

Officer Dade gave us an arched–eyebrow look that was half suspicion and half amusement. We waited until she left before collapsing into middle school giggles.

We ended the meeting in a circle: holding hands, and reciting the Serenity Prayer: *Grant me the Serenity to accept the things I cannot change, Courage to change the things I can, And the Wisdom to know the difference.*

I wondered if I would have the courage to face the rest of my life in prison.

I didn't sleep much that night. I kept seeing their faces. I don't know what I expected when I went into the prison. As I said, I didn't think much about it. But meeting the women made the project far more than just another gig. I'd only been with them for ninety minutes, and already I was feeling their pain and seeing their beauty. What I did not expect was their normalness. The women are all of us: daughters, sisters, wives, mothers and, saddest of all, kids.

I did not expect some of them would become dear friends.

CHAPTER TWO:
Developing the Play

The women talk and write

Regular meetings for I–WISH are twice a month, the second and fourth Thursdays. This gave me two weeks to formulate a plan. I hit on an idea. One of my favorite shows is *The Me Nobody Knows*, a 1970s rock musical inspired by Stephen M. Joseph's book, *Children's Voices from the Ghetto*, an anthology of writings from two hundred New York City students. The production won an Obie (the off–Broadway award) and two Broadway Tonys. Another good book/play is *The Spoon River Anthology*, written in 1915 by Edgar Lee Master, a collection of writings that reveals the goings on in the fictional town of Spoon River.

Could we use the same formats? Let each woman tell her story—her hopes, her dreams, her regrets, her thoughts? Allow people to see them for who they are rather than what they had done? As convicted criminals, they are known only for the acts they committed on the worst day of their lives. What about the rest of their lives—before and after? Who were they? And, just as important: Who are they now?

I have a teacher friend. Brilliant. Energetic. The kids love her. Always coming up with creative projects to make learning fun. On one particularly frustrating day, she muttered an obscene word. A kid heard it, told his parents, the school board got involved, and she was fired. From then on all her accomplishments vanished. When her name came up, she was, "the teacher who dropped the f–bomb."

Of course, murder is not the same as mumbling a dirty word, but the principle applies. These women had lives before whatever circumstances led them to their desperate acts. They were wives and mothers and secretaries and waitresses and professional women—and high school students. Several women in our group are college graduates and one is a former professor with three PhDs. All that is erased. Each woman is now a number and she is defined by her crime: "the one who killed her husband/father/boyfriend/romantic rival…." I wanted people to see the woman who still resided inside the convicted felon.

I wasn't sure how the idea would go over with the women. After the first meeting, several of the younger women had taken me aside.

"We really want a story," a tall twenty–something said. She flicked long dreadlocks over her shoulder. "And I want a big part."

"I had a lot of lines in the play we did," a thirty–something said. "Everybody said I was the best one in the play."

Some things are the same in or out of a prison.

I had directed productions of *The Me Nobody Knows* and *The Spoon River Anthology,* so I had both scripts. I got permission to take the books into the prison, along with a bigger notebook, pens, and a few more pencils.

I told the women that after listening to them and hearing about their lives, I didn't think they needed comedy to reach the kids; they needed honesty. I told them I believed the kids had to see *them,* see the kids the women once were. And the kids needed to see themselves in the women—especially those experiencing pain of the same kind. I read a few excerpts from *The Me Nobody Knows* and *Spoon River* out loud and told them my idea.

The women who wanted "big parts" were not happy with the plan. They turned out to be emerging divas. They wanted a story. Period. In truth, they wanted to be the stars of a story. If we went with my idea, there would be no "big parts." Anyone who wanted to participate could, and the parts would be equal. Most, however, were willing to give it a try.

I asked the women to write anything and everything that came into their heads. I gave them writing prompts for inspiration; other than that, they were on their own. We spent more time talking about prison life. I took notes and, later, incorporated some of our conversations into the play. I told them during the play development process we would have acting classes (a few groans: "That Russian guy again?"). I sent them back to their cells with instructions to have some pieces ready for me at the next meeting.

Two weeks later I was delighted to find many of the women had taken the assignment to heart. They handed me sheaves of paper. I promised to read their work over the next two weeks. We continued our conversations about their lives. The more they talked, the more they opened up. They were eager to share their stories, often interrupting one another in their attempt to help me understand what life in prison really meant—what they wanted kids to know. It was fascinating, and more and more I was struck by the courage they had to have just to get through another day.

When I got home, I started reading a few of the pieces they had written. I intended to just look them over, but I ended up reading all night. The women had poured out their souls, sometimes writing about events or feelings they had never shared. Many of the essays started with, "I've never told anyone this, but…"

They wrote of their childhoods, their memories, their feelings, their pasts, presents, and futures, their regrets, their feelings of guilt and remorse, and their hopes. I spent that night and more crying over the handwritten pages, torn between my fondness for these desperate women and sympathy for their victims and for their victims' families. It was difficult to reconcile the villainous mug shots in the newspapers with the creative, intelligent people who had written with such eloquence.

By this time Circus Camp was in full swing and I was leading a somewhat contradictory existence. The prison warden, Brenda Shell–Eleazer, had given us permission to meet twice a week to work on the production. By day I was in a circus atmosphere, surrounded by adorable children excited about learning to ride a unicycle or juggle three balls. By night I was immersed in a world of desperate people, some so depressed I didn't know how they managed to get up in the morning. On meeting nights I barely had time to get to rehearsal after circus camp, so I had to wear my bright red circus T–shirt. It always seemed out of place in the prison.

When I had received about a dozen submissions, I began to put the play together. I decided on ten scenes:

1. Introduction
2. Childhood
3. Growing up
4. High School
5. Adult Life
6. Crime
7. Trial and Sentencing
8. Prison Life
9. The Future
10. Advice

I sorted out the writings. Some were pages long, as if once the women started writing they couldn't stop. I edited the lengthier ones, put them into their various categories, and added a beginning and an end. By the time I finished, I had about twenty minutes' worth of material. Not enough for a play, but a good start. I typed them all up, put them in binders, and got permission to take the binders into the prison.

We spent the next meeting doing a read–through of the play's beginnings. I'm happy to report it was a hit. Even the divas who wanted the "big parts" approved, albeit with a bit of reluctance. We discussed who would say what, but I convinced them we had to have more material and the play had to be finished before we assigned lines.

At the following meeting a stack of papers greeted me. Everyone wanted to get in on the act. With the outline complete, it was easier to categorize the writings. But now I was faced with another problem: the writings were so heavy and so gut wrenching I was afraid audience members might throw up before the play was over. So, in an ironic twist, it fell to me to add comedy to lighten the script. I wrote a couple of poems and a rap on drugs and threw in an amusing scene comparing prison to high school.

It came time to assign lines. As the director, I assumed that was my job. Wrong. The women grabbed the script and ran with it. Some wanted to say the lines they had written; others did not, preferring anonymity. It usually takes me hours to assign roles in a multicast show. The women accomplished it in thirty minutes.

So we had a play. A play with no name. We bandied about many suggestions: *Voices from Behind Bars. We Are Not Invisible. We Are Here.* It was Amanda, the former college professor, who came up with the answer.

"We are invisible," she said. "We want people to see us. I think we should call the play: FACES."

CHAPTER THREE:
The Rehearsal Process

Frustration and triumph

By the end of July we were ready to start rehearsal. A few of the women had been in plays in elementary school and one had been in a high school performance. Other than that, we started from scratch. I knew I had to work with each actor, so I made a schedule of small scene rehearsals with four or five people at a time.

That's when the trouble started and that's when some of the women decided I wasn't quite as nice as I appeared to be. Truth be told, when I put on the director's hat, I'm not. When I direct a show I have a mantra: *I want to hear your suggestions, but if we disagree, we compromise and do it my way.* I learned long ago that anything bad or anything that goes wrong in a show is the director's fault. If I'm going to be blamed, it's going to be for something I did. I explained my philosophy and they agreed to it—to a point.

We started with diction. The evening progressed from amusing to hilarious, with lots of wisecracks and laughter.

Me: There is no such animal as a do— or a ca—. It's do**g** and ca**t**. Finish your words. Open your mouth.

Them: My mouth *is* open! See? Aaaaaaaaaaah.

Me: I want to see your teeth!

Them: Whatareyouadentist?

And then came the tongue twisters:

Me: Repeat after me: Betty Botter bought some butter…

Them: Biddy Booter butte sum bidder…

Me: Rubber baby buggy bumpers

Them: Rubber baggy bubby bempers

Me: Toy boat, Toy boat. Toy boat.

Them: Toy boat. Toy butt. Tu boit. Damn!

Me: Don't drop your voice at the end of a sentence. Keep your voice up. Pronounce your words correctly. Enunciate. Watch your phrasing. Be aware of timing. Slow down!

Them: You

Want

Slow?

How's

This?

On to stage directions:

Me: Downstage is the front of the stage; upstage is the back.

Them: Why?

Me: Because the Greeks said so.

Them: Are you Greek?

Me: No.

Them: Neither am I.

Me: When standing profile, slip your downstage foot slightly behind your upstage foot so you are more open to the audience. It's called cheating.

Them: Cheating is what got me here in the first place. (Followed by loud guffaws.)

Me: Don't turn your back. Keep your head up. Make eye contact.

Them: That's creepy.

Me: Don't just say the words. Believe what you're saying. Make your audience believe it. Remember Stanislavski: What do you *do* when you are remembering a beautiful flower or an adorable puppy? What do you *do* when you want people to really hear what you are saying? Do the actions. Evoke your response.

Them: The actions make me cry.

Me: Good.

Over and over again, until it was no longer amusing or hilarious. What had started out as fun and games was turning into repetitive, difficult, boring work.

"You're trying to turn us into professional actors," they yelled at me.

"Yup," I said.

"It's not fair. It's too hard."

I sympathized with them. Acting is hard work. But hard work means you work harder. The complaining went on for a couple of weeks. It turned into a war. Several threatened to quit; none did. Finally, they adopted a mantra of their own: *If we can help just one kid, all our work will be worth it.* Most of them pitched in and worked their buns off.

However, divas always find something to complain about and this group was no different.

A lot of their actions were passive–aggressive. A call to get started was met with, "Yeah, in a minute." An off–book rehearsal, when they were supposed to have their lines memorized, became time to sneak scripts on stage. I had a solution for that: during the "Yeah, in a minute" pauses, I walked around the room and confiscated the scripts. That just made the divas angrier.

Sometimes the conflict got downright nasty: "I've already said the line twice. I'm not saying it again." Some walkouts. Phony excuses for missing rehearsal: "I have to get my hair done."

I'm embarrassed to admit I tolerated the bad behavior far longer than I should have. I felt pity for them so I put up with it. It took me a while to realize this was the most disrespectful response of all.

Most of the time, however, it was just plain fun. When it came time to choose the music, I had pieces all picked out and my CDs laid out in a row. I tend to go more with the classical or Broadway/pop route. The women weren't having much of that. Somehow they managed to run back and forth to their cells, loading me down with CDs and telling me which music went with which scene.

That was a fun night. The women bellowed out every song they played. A lot of wild dancing was involved, too. Their choices were much better than mine—the only ones I even heard of were Michael Jackson and Mary J. Blige. Every piece they picked out was perfect, although they did allow me to keep in Bach's Toccata and Fugue in D minor to introduce the crime scene and Cyndi Lauper's hit song, "Girls Just Want to Have Fun," to kick off the high school scene. I was grateful for that.

I met with each small group twice, once to analyze the lines and give suggestions about delivery, and a second time to polish. Then it came time for full company rehearsals.

I didn't know it when I wrote that little scene about prison versus high school, but prison life *is* a lot like high school life. Sometimes it's more like middle school. Many of the inmates were in prison because they started doing drugs at a young age. Psychiatrists and psychologists say people on drugs are unable to pay much attention to emotional and social growth. I believe them. I found that some of the women had simply stopped maturing; their mentality was more adolescent than adult. They had cliques and people they didn't like and wouldn't speak to or sit next to. Blocking the group, I sat one woman next to someone she didn't like. She refused to sit in that spot.

She crossed her arms and looked up at the ceiling. "No. I don't like her. I won't sit there." The only thing missing was a pouting lower lip.

I moved her. She didn't like that seatmate, either, and sulked for the entire rehearsal.

Maybe it is to be expected. When one is told when to get up, when to eat, when to go to the bathroom, when to bathe, and when to go to bed, it must be difficult to continue on the road to emotional maturation.

As a result of their immaturity, physical fights among inmates sometimes break out, although not as often and usually not as violent as the stabbings and killings in a men's prison. Fortunately, while there were disagreements, arguments, and catty exchanges during our rehearsals and performances, no actual fights occurred. But sometimes, when I got to rehearsal, one of the younger members would be missing.

"Where's Patty?" I would ask.

A casual explanation would follow. "She got into a fight. She's on lock."

Lock—also known as segregation or "seg"—means an inmate is sent to an isolation barrack and confined to her cell. One hour out of every forty–eight she is allowed out to shower and exercise. No jobs. No school. No phone calls or visits except for lawyers and clergy. No chance to see her friends.

Any appliances she had in her former cell are left behind—none permitted in lock. No TV. Her meals are served through a locked slot in the middle of the door: slipped in and out—no contact allowed. She is permitted to have soap, but no oils or lotions; they can be used to slick the locks. This is a difficult deprivation for the African–American women; they depend on the moisturizers to groom their hair.

According to the women, the lock unit is noisy. The confined prisoners often sleep all day and spend their night screaming their frustrations and fighting with one another through the walls.

The sentences are specific: a number of days—or weeks—or months—or years. The length of the sentence depends upon the severity of the infraction, but the slightest violation can result in a "ticket," a conviction, and some lock time. And a high number of tickets or convictions can have a drastic negative influence on appeals for parole.

Even small infractions are considered "a threat to the security of the institution." At one rehearsal I mentioned it was my birthday. Danielle asked me for a piece of notebook paper. As we rehearsed, she doodled on the paper and, as I was leaving, presented me with a delightful birthday greeting. I thanked her and put it in my notebook.

Several months later, one of the gatehouse officers examined my notebook and found the paper. "What is this?"

I smiled. "It's a birthday card. One of the women made it for me. Isn't it pretty?"

She jabbed her index finger at the paper "You are not permitted to accept anything from the inmates."

"But it's a birthday card."

Hands on her hips, she repeated the edict. "You are not permitted to accept anything from the inmates."

I tried to make light of it. "Well, technically I didn't receive it from her. I gave her the piece of paper and she handed it back."

She shook her finger at me. "You are not permitted to give anything to the inmates. You are threatening the security of this institution. This is going to be reported. It will go on her record." She confiscated the birthday card.

I was terrified. Was Danielle going to be in trouble? Would her thoughtful gesture result in time on lock and affect her prison record?

When I got inside, I went directly to one of the senior officers. I told him it was entirely my fault and to please not punish Danielle. I'm glad to say he took care of the problem and there were no repercussions for my friend.

This may sound like an overreaction on the gatehouse officer's part, but I came to understand that the rules for the staff are just as stringent as the rules for the inmates. This is a maximum–security prison. One small lapse in security can result in harm to another inmate, an escape, violence toward victims and witnesses, a return to criminal behavior, revenge killings, and headlines in the newspapers. For the officers it can mean demotion or job loss.

Lorna joined the cast late in the run after release from a term on lock. Incarcerated for eight years, she had been confined to lock, on and off, for five of those years because of multiple escape attempts.

At a Christmas party I met a man who worked for the county's sanitation department. When I told him I worked at the prison, he said. "Yeah? That's part of my route. One time, I was picking up a dumpster and a leg came out."

"That was Lorna," I said.

I thought this was pretty funny until Brenda told me several officers had been fired after the incident. They not only lost their jobs, they lost their family's health insurance and pension benefits as well. Lorna didn't make any escape attempts during the short time she was in the show, but I have no doubt she will try again. The officers keep a close eye on her.

The threat of lock, however, does not keep the inmates from trying to outwit the establishment. They have so many rules and regulations that "getting away with something" is, I think, a predictable response, however stupid or risky it may be. I think it is comparable to defiant acts in the "outside world." In response to authority, elementary school kids play with soap bubbles in the restroom; middle school kids pass clandestine notes; high schoolers hide cell phones in their socks; and good, solid citizens cheat on their income taxes.

Any time a woman leaves her cell the door is locked. One day, Sally, another one of the younger inmates, didn't want to have to wait for the officers to open her door when she returned from the shower. She stuck a sock in the door to keep it from locking. She was caught, charged with an escape attempt, and sentenced to segregation. She missed a number of performances.

All of us really missed her. The cast members got up a petition, signed it, and sent it to the warden, begging for leniency. Brenda excused Sally from the last few days of her sentence so she could be in later shows. Sally came rushing into the run–through rehearsal the day before the performance and hugged everyone. "I was dying!" she said. As far as I know, she never stuck a sock in her door again.

Sometimes I didn't understand why the women got upset over things that, to me, were of little consequence. One day the commissary closed. It was only closed for that one day. I couldn't help but think: *What's the big deal?*

Except it *was* a big deal. They only get to go to commissary once a week. If it is closed on your day, you have to wait until the following week. If you are out of toothpaste or deodorant, that can be a mighty long week.

Danielle wrote about how much she missed biscuits.

> True feelings and thoughts can sometimes wreck your brain, from watching a cooking show on TV to using the bathroom. I was watching a cooking show and wondering to myself: damn, will I ever be able to taste a biscuit again or eat a Bar–B–Q spare rib? How about a steak or a crab cake?

I heard that biscuit line multiple times in rehearsals and shows before it registered with me: she's talking about ordinary old biscuits. I asked her about it:

"Do you really miss biscuits that much?"

She glanced away with a memory smile. She looked back at me and laughed, but her eyes were misty. "I haven't had a biscuit in fourteen years," she told me. "If I ever get out of here, the first thing I will do is eat a biscuit."

The next time I had a biscuit, I looked at it for a long time.

Sometimes the divas' antics annoyed everyone. I was working hard and most of the women were, too. I had to remind myself—and others—that only a few were being difficult although, as all teachers know, it only takes a few to make life unpleasant.

I think the low point came when one of the actors was talking during my post–rehearsal notes to the cast. I asked her to be quiet and she got offended. She said, "How could you speak to me like that? I'm the one who defends you." She walked out.

I was stunned. I couldn't figure out why I needed to be defended. Still haven't. True, I expected a lot from them, but I was never disrespectful. Then again, I know an actor's second favorite indoor sport is complaining about the director—another thing that is the same in or out of a prison.

There is an alternate possibility: Some of the nasty comments the divas directed at me were much like insults teenagers hurl at their mothers: "That's stupid," "You don't know what you're talking about," "You're not the boss of me," "Why are you picking on me," "No. I'm not going to rehearse now. I'm not in the mood."—would have resulted in lock time if they said the same thing to an officer. They knew I would not report them. Maybe I was a safety net for thoughts they didn't dare say out loud elsewhere.

A battle ensued between the divas, who threatened to quit because I was "too demanding," and the more mature women, who threatened to quit because they were embarrassed by their colleagues' childish behavior. They felt the divas' actions reflected on them. Lots of angry exchanges and apoplectic glances flew around the rehearsal space.

Why didn't I quit? In the first place, divas are a part of the theatrical world: with one exception (Chapter Eight), I've never been part of a show that didn't have at least one. In the second place, there's the show business credo: You don't walk out on a show, no matter what. And third: just plain stubbornness.

So we plugged on. We set our opening for October, four months after our first meeting.

We had to have a crew. I figured we needed one for sound; two side coaches ready to prompt missed cues or forgotten lines, one house manager, and two for spot. We needed two on the spotlight because the lines came thick and fast; the operator wouldn't have time to look at the script. Someone had to call the cues and let her know who was up next.

I announced our crew needs at a rehearsal. I guess show biz fever had caught on: six volunteers showed up before the next day was out. Laticia, twenty–eight years old and incarcerated for four years, was our "sound engineer" (her self–endowed title). The first thing I did was to teach her the elements of sound: fading in, fading out, matching sound levels to voice and mood… She took to it right away and, as far as I know, never missed a cue.

In my favorite mental video of Laticia, she is playing with a black Labrador puppy. The prison has a service dog program. Professional handlers assign a dog to individual inmates for basic training: housebreaking, sit, stay, heel…, and then the dogs are turned over to experts who train them to assist the handicapped. Danielle was working with the Labrador and would bring him to rehearsal. Laticia romped with the puppy, rolled on the floor, and laughed as he licked her face. In my mind, she looks every inch the lovely woman–child she is.

The spotlight was another matter. I brought in my followspot, which is not one of the nice, new, sleek, lightweight modern followspots. I bought my spotlight thirty years ago—used. Very used. It is a huge monstrosity that may have lit Bob Hope in his early vaudeville days.

Shanna, the designated operator, twenty–seven years old, in prison since she was in tenth grade, looked at it and said, "I'm supposed to work that thing?" But she was game. I taught her the basics and, when there was a pause in rehearsals, she would practice hitting a mark with a pinpoint of light. She got so good she could hit every actor with the light on the first try—not easy when the performers are crowded together.

Two weeks into production Shanna was late to a performance. I took over the spot. Ten minutes into the show she came rushing in. "Get away from my spot. You don't know what you're doing." She hip–bumped me out of the way. How we laughed.

Rehearsing in the gym was different from rehearsing in the smaller rooms. The gym is big—lots of room to spread out. Exercise machines line the walls, creating lots of places for people to sit away from our "stage," otherwise known as bleachers. The actors would disperse from one end of the gym to the other, with my little divas making it plain they would take part in rehearsal when they were good and ready and not one moment sooner.

I had gotten over my "Oh, the poor things are in jail" pity party. This time I didn't ignore their actions. I was mad and I let them know it. Lots of harrumphs and indignant faces met my loud and angry, "We are going to start NOW!" I didn't care. We never began on time, but we always had to finish on time because of the blessed "count."

I came to hate the word *count* almost as much as the women did. A count is required at the beginning of every shift: 7 A.M., 3 P.M., and 11 P.M. All movement in the prison is stopped. And the count must be perfect. If one inmate isn't where she is supposed to be, the entire prison shuts down. She might be in a doctor's office or the bathroom, but she must be located. Count can take thirty minutes or two hours.

Sometimes there are surprise counts in the middle of the night. The women have to get out of bed, stand by their cell doors, and show their badges. They tell me they often can't get back to sleep after a middle–of–the–night count. Fortunately, we never had a count during a show, but we did have several during rehearsals, which took away precious time.

The week before opening, we had our own version of Production Week, affectionately referred to by the theatrical community as "Hell Week." We rehearsed every night until 9 P.M., late for the women since they have to be up at 4:30 A.M., so they can get breakfast and be at their jobs by 7 A.M., so they can be off at 2 P.M., and back in their cells in time for the almighty count.

That's another thing that took me by surprise. One of the most frustrating things about directing a show is actors who don't show up for rehearsal. A performer's assurance, "Don't worry. I know my part," makes me want to climb a wall. To me, this means she is completely disregarding other performers and not recognizing the effort it takes to develop timing, flow, build, and interaction with other characters. One thought I had going into the project was: at least they'll be available for rehearsal. A real captive audience. (Sorry.)

But the women not only have day jobs with strict accountability for their hours, they have evening activities as well: book clubs, Bible study, religious services, GED classes (General Educational Development courses to earn a Certificate of High School Equivalency), college classes, yoga, Pilates… the list goes on. Most of the classes are taught by volunteers or by the inmates themselves.

For the women who serve shorter sentences—ninety percent of the population—these classes are invaluable. Often they leave prison better prepared to enter the job market than they were in their former lives. This cuts down considerably on recidivism:

> The rate at which ex–inmates are returned to prison or put on probation for new crimes within three years of release stood at 40.5 percent in 2012, an almost 3 percent drop from the previous year and almost 11 percent lower than in 2000, when the state's recidivism rate stood at 51.4 percent… Secretary Gary D. Maynard, the top official at the Department of Public Safety and Correctional Services, credited the prison system's improved educational and job skills training programs, as well as stronger partnerships with state agencies that provide medical and mental health services to inmates and upon their release.[2]

For the lifers it is an opportunity to improve their minds and an expression of hope.

The most important event, of course, is visiting hours. Visitors are the women's lifelines to the outside world and an automatic excuse for missing rehearsal. Nothing means more

---

[2]"Ex–offenders less likely to return to prison, Maryland officials say" by Justin George, *The Baltimore Sun*. September 30, 2013.

to these women than spending time with a loved one. Many of them are mothers and they try hard to maintain a relationship with their children.

As with every show, we had to have at least one technical rehearsal. This meant the actors had to take their places and blah–blah through their lines while the crew and I went through the light and sound cues. It's boring for everyone and, of course, a perfect excuse for our divas to vent.

"I don't see why we have to be here wasting our time while they fool around with the spot light and the sound equipment," they said to each other.

A nasty thought crossed my mind: *Time is one thing you have plenty of.* I didn't say it out loud—an exercise in self–control.

We used my CD player for the music and the prison's sound system for the microphones. The system is a nightmare: an antiquated jumble of questionable amplifiers and oversized speakers that probably predate my followspot. Darcy, our amazing vocalist, took charge of it; Laticia and I were glad to leave it in her hands. The prison has four microphones; I brought in two of mine. The cables were constantly tangled and squeaks and squawks were abundant, but Darcy kept everything under control—most of the time.

The final night of Hell Week we presented a preview to the three most important people involved in initiating the project: Warden Brenda Shell–Eleazer, Mary Pat, and Susan. I didn't know how it would go. We had made it through the play only once—constantly interrupted by one thing or another. We had never had a rehearsal with the entire cast present. I knew the play had great potential, but could the women pull it off?

Stage fright spread through the group like fungus in a locker room. The most important questions concerned Brenda: "What will Warden Shell think? Will she like it? Will she be proud of us?" Of course they cared about Mary Pat and Susan's opinions, but they especially wanted approval from the woman most important in their lives.

I was shaking a bit as well. Most of the women had worked so hard. I wanted a triumph for them. I wanted them to be as proud of themselves as I was of them.

Brenda, Susan, and Mary Pat took their seats. I started the come–in music, crossed my fingers, and sent Stanislavski a quick plea for help.

CHAPTER FOUR:
The Preview Show

Pre–show jitters

The gym is a stark place. Gray–green walls almost match the inmates' gray prison issue outfits. Like all gymnasiums, it is a rectangle, but the far long wall opposite from the entrance is a continuous line of three giant steps of cement bleachers. Our performance area was at the center of those bleachers. I set it up that way so we could have the elements of staging: groups and levels.

This meant, however, the spotlight only had a throw of the width of the gym, which resulted in a small diameter of beamed light. For a full group spot, I had to cram the twenty–three actors into a space less than twenty feet wide. This, of course, gave the divas something else to complain about.

"Why do we have to be so crowded?"

"Because I want you in the light."

"I don't want to be in the light. It's too hot."

Sigh.

As the come–in music played: Mary J. Blige's heartbreaking autobiographical anthem, "No More Drama," I checked on the performers. They were on line outside the door, chewing their nails and making last trips to the bathroom. I wished them all luck and we had a group hug—

even the divas joined in. I told them they were going to be wonderful and hoped I was right. They were on their own.

I returned to the gym. Mary J. Blige's incredibly beautiful vocal had set the mood. It was time to begin. I asked the officers to douse the house lights. This doesn't mean complete darkness—not in a prison.

I faded out the music and the cast and crew filed through the semidarkness in eerie silence. The cast took their places on stage; the crew took their assigned positions.

Their costumes looked wonderful. Some of the women work in the sewing room—those orange reflective vests we see on Maryland highways are made in the prison. With permission, they used spare and outdated material to make jumpsuits of various styles: some one–piece, some shirts and pants. Most were the typical orange; others were white with black letters. Some of the women put horizontal black stripes on them just for fun. They printed numbers on the breast pockets: their birthdays, their kids' birthdays, numbers that had meaning only to them… they showed a fun, creative spark.

They took their places on the bleachers. Every one of them looked beautiful. How I wished I could take just one picture. I cued Laticia for the introductory music—a haunting urban instrumental. Thirty seconds into the piece, Laticia faded out the music at just the right place and Sheila stood to deliver the play's introduction:

> Good evening. We are glad you are here. We are not glad we are here.
> I am prisoner #_____.
> But I am more than a number. I am a person.
> And I used to be a teenager, just like you…

The play flowed. It was perfect. It was magic. A few mistakes here and there, but they didn't matter. I watched the women. No hunched backs, no faces staring at the floor. They were wonderful and they knew it. They were in the moment. They were proud. For one hour and five minutes, they were free.

I looked over at Brenda, Mary Pat, and Susan. They were riveted to their seats. If they moved at all—except to applaud boisterously—I didn't see it. They cried, they laughed. They clasped their hands. They knew they were witnessing a miracle. I have been in show business my entire life. I defy any Broadway director to see these women and not declare them consummate professionals.

Our three guests were on their feet before the curtain call even began. They applauded until the play–off music faded. Then they applauded some more.

"Did you really like it?" I heard one of the women ask Brenda.

"I loved it. You were wonderful!"

"Did you *really* like it?" another woman said.

I fully expected one of them to grab a microphone and shout, "They like us! They really like us!"

More hugs, more congratulations, more kudos, and then the officers rushed them out of the gymnasium. The magic had ended and they had to be back in their cells in time for count.

CHAPTER FIVE:
We Open to the Public

Standing ovations and letters of praise

Our first public presentation was six days later. Before the show we holed up in a room down the hall from the entrance to the gym. The women were nervous, but not as much as they had been for our preview performance. The chatter concerned more mundane things, nothing about upset stomachs or sweaty palms. It was like any other backstage: the younger actors practiced their rap; the older actors checked their makeup, and the divas sat in a corner and complained about...something.

These were the same depressed women I had met four months earlier, except, at least for the moment, they weren't quite so depressed. They were standing straighter, sitting taller, proud of what they were doing, pride that comes from knowing you are damn good.

Getting the audience in was no easy matter. Just as I have to go through clearance whenever I go into the prison, so did every audience member. We had a hundred people at that first performance—later the allowed number was reduced to fifty. Each person had to submit his or her birth date and Social Security number in advance for a background check—a lot of work for the administration.

The gatehouse is small—certainly not enough space for a hundred people. Mary Pat and Susan ran their legs off greeting our guests and helping the officers escort them in—one small group at a time. The gatehouse officers had a guest list. Every guest had to go through the security search process, get checked in, turn in their ID's, and be issued a visitor's pass—in this case a plastic bracelet. Upon their exits, the bracelets would be cut off their wrists, gathered into a pile, and counted.

We had asked everyone to be at the prison by 6 P.M. and we had warned them of the restrictions—especially the ban against underwire bras. One of the women didn't get the memo and had to leave her bra in her car. She was instructed to keep her arms crossed over her chest because the gym was cold.

The guests went through the same clanging doors I described above, a new experience for almost all of them. We have talked about producing the play on the outside with professional actors, but the biggest problem would be recreating the prison ambience. There is no doubt it was a major factor in the play's success—that, and the fact the lives the women were describing were their own.

After the audience members completed the trek through the endless doors, officers led them down two short flights of stairs. The gym is across from the dining hall; the residual odors of that evening's meal still lingered—not always the most pleasant of smells (canned peas are the worst).

As house manager, Amirra had supervised the setup of the folding chairs—multiple rows with an aisle down the middle. One of the divas started to help, but got mad and quit when I insisted the chairs be staggered to provide sightlines.

Sigh.

Our guests took their seats and sat in silence, intimidated by the gray–green walls and the cadre of uniformed officers. There was no audience buzz, one of my favorite things in the preshow world. Again, Mary J. Blige's lilting voice filled the quiet and set the mood.

The performance was supposed to start at 7 P.M. We finally got our audience settled in by 7:30. The women were lined up in the upper hallway where there are small windows that look down into the gym. The reality of performing for a bunch of strangers hit home. Nail chewing and trips to the bathroom resumed. I stayed with them and tried to joke them out of it, but they kept glancing down at the crowd. I hugged them all and reminded them how wonderful they had been in the preview performance.

"That was different," one of them said. "These are real people."

"Does that make Warden Shell, Mary Pat, and Susan unreal people?" I asked her.

She laughed a little at my pathetic joke and went back to staring through the window.

But I knew what she meant. These "real people" scared me a little, too. I had no idea how they would react to the women. Would they be judgmental? Would they see the beauty? Would they see the courage it took for these women to bare their souls in front of strangers?

Sheila went through the introductory lines. Nobody in the audience moved. If I listened closely, I could hear breathing—nothing more. No one moved. No one coughed. They seemed to sense the performance they were about to see would be nothing like anything they had ever experienced. What would they think of that experience? What would they think of the women?

I needn't have worried. The women spun their magic around these strangers just as they had around Brenda, Mary Pat, and Susan. Applause came in the right places, and so did laughter—and tears.

Following Darcy's solo, "Waiting for My Child to Come Home," sung *a cappella*, there was dead silence. Darcy look puzzled—and hurt. She didn't understand this was the highest compliment an audience can give a performer. They were literally stunned into silence by her haunting voice wafting through the gray–green gymnasium, bouncing off the cement walls, and echoing around the room. Her beautiful smile reappeared when thunderous applause broke out.

Usually a standing ovation starts with a few people and spreads through the audience. Not this time. As one, a hundred people rose to their feet before the women had even finished the unison recitation of the final line, "I am a person. Just like you." The performers took their curtain call with pride, acknowledging their audience's response with dignity.

I only wished Jerry could have been there. He would have been as proud of the women as I was. He would have been proud of me, too.

We had decided to have a question–and–answer session following each performance. Again, I had no idea how this would work out. What if the questions were hurtful? What if there were no questions? Just as before, all my fears were baseless, except most members of the audience only wanted to congratulate the women on their incredible performance and thank them for allowing them into their lives.

Mary Pat ended the Q and A session with thanks to the guests. We expected them to prepare for the complex route back to the outside. Instead, they rushed to the stage area to embrace the women. Many were in tears, wishing there were something they could do to take away the women's pain. Small talk and more congratulations followed the initial emotional outburst. No one wanted to leave.

Other than the fact we were in a maximum–security prison, enclosed by gray–green walls, surrounded by uniformed officers, and the performers were convicted murderers who had to be hurried out of the gym to prepare for count, it was just like any ordinary post–opening show celebration.

These are just a few of the many congratulatory letters we received:

From a social worker:

> As a social worker for the Public Defender's
> Office Juvenile Protection Division, I believe that

the play would be of great benefit for at–risk teens. As a clinical social worker, I also see the value in allowing inmates expression of painful feelings and previous experiences. I believe that no matter what our status, we all as human beings need to believe that we contribute to society. This great endeavor helps the inmates to become less egocentric and more serving of others. I am also a volunteer for the Narcotics Anonymous meeting at [the prison]. Often the theme of [many of the performers] involved the dangers of substance use and the impact [the drugs had] on their lives. This is one of the factors that leads to recidivism and often death. I believe that you and your team are doing worthwhile work and [will] have an impact on both recidivism and harmony within the institution.

From a community leader:

I was fortunate to have the opportunity to see a performance of FACES last June. I was very moved by it and will never forget it. Betty May produced and directed an impressive performance. I am a volunteer with Voices for Children, and serve as a CASA (Court–Appointed Special Advocate) for abused and neglected children. I hope that the performances of FACES will continue. Many in our community should have the opportunity to see and hear these women talk about their lives and their aspirations. It is important to establish a connection between women in prison and our community. This type of performance is valuable both to the women in the drama and to members of the audience. In my opinion, it would be especially relevant to present to high school girls.

From a lay minister:

The play is indeed great [with] powerful messages for the general population as well as teenagers. I serve as coordinator of women volunteers at [another prison] and minister to the detainees. I have met women of all ages, levels of education, [and] socio–economic status. I also volunteer at a local Crisis Center and am a member of the Outreach and Advocacy committee at my church. Since attending the performance, I have been waiting for word of future dates so that I might make others ... aware of FACES. In my opinion, at least bi–monthly performances would be required to reach the many who would benefit from [the production].
Good luck and God's blessings on your mission.

From a youth group leader:

I took several teenagers and their parents to the play and it was profound. The girls didn't take their eyes off the play the entire time and the tears in their eyes were the true feelings they acquired from such a moving and "real" performance. The play is something that I suggest everyone have the opportunity to see: the young, the teens, the old. I had one parent turn to me and just related so well to [an inmate] who was molested while growing up. She felt this particular part...so strongly that I could feel her pain as if it jumped on my back.... This play brought a mother of five to feel what she hadn't in a long time, yet needed to. She called me the next day thanking me for inviting her to the play. She said [neither] she nor the other mother who attended could get the performance out of their heads.

I remember one of the young girls calling her mother after we got into the car after the play and, with much excitement and enthusiasm, [telling] her mother how this play affected her. How these are real people with a story to their life and how well she understood the entire play. Then she proceeded to tell her mother that after the play we got to hug the women and how nice these women are. She was so glad to have seen the play and couldn't get it out of her mind the entire evening, into the next day. She kept talking about it the entire ride home and just felt bad, yet realized how nice her own life is. This performance has the ability to force others to think about other people. To envision a different life and the heartache many women who are incarcerated experience can indeed be very moving.

When the young teenagers walked into the front door of the prison to see the play, the change from when they walked out was incredible. Fear, nervousness, uncertainty walking in — [then] seeing that these were real people who experienced much pain in their lives and how they didn't want to make poor choices, too. The empathy and care were evident, and the gratefulness towards their own lives grew at that moment.

I strongly suggest this play be shown again and opened to all school aged children/young adults [and] to senior citizens. I would love to see it again.

From a religious leader:

I found the play profoundly moving. One of the great values was that it [helped] the audience to realize that becoming incarcerated could happen to anyone, and to get to know the real stories and life experiences of those who are currently incarcerated. The content, artistic form of the play and the quality of the women's performance made it profoundly moving.

I pray that FACES will continue to be presented. Unfortunately [the] women cannot travel to other sites but I pray that they can speak from [the prison] to help the larger world become better informed of how greatly we need to support rehabilitation and transitional services for incarcerated men and women, for their own sake and for the sake of our civic community, as well as to work to prevent teenagers from becoming incarcerated.

Many thanks for all that you are doing.

From a chaplain:

I have never seen a more powerful presentation and I am not making that statement as a cliché or just for effect. What makes this play so powerful is the actors are playing themselves and no one can portray YOU better than YOU. Whatever they do is genuine and it comes across as such. This play is more effective and real than the Scared Straight Program because it also dramatizes the hurt as well as the rigors of prison life. This is a great deterrent for juveniles and young women who think going to prison is not the end of their freedom. There is nothing glorious about this production except the strength, willingness, honesty, and sacrifice of the women who have bared their souls to help somebody. May God bless them all and make a way for this play to continue to perpetuate healing, deliverance, and forgiveness.

From a church member:

I think about the play often as though I have just seen it on yesterday. I thought that it was breathtaking and should be used as a tool to help others. We serve a forgiving God who forgives us daily once we repent. Those ladies have been forgiven although having to pay the consequences for their wrong doings and have been given a second chance to be a testimony to others to make wise choices. I feel that anyone who would try to put a stop to this play being performed would do a disservice to so many people. Please give the ladies a chance to redeem themselves. We look on the outer appearance but God looks upon the heart.

From a government employee:

This memo is being written because in my heart I believe it is worth sharing. On Friday, May 15, 2009 I had an opportunity along with my sister and brother–in–law to visit [the prison]. Being employed with the Office of the Public Defender has afforded me opportunities that otherwise would not have been extended to me.
We did not know what to expect as we entered the prison. Upon being cleared, we were escorted into the gym where we took our seats. I must say that it was kind of eerie sitting waiting for the play to begin. As we looked back, there were about 20 women who entered dressed in orange jump suits with numbers written on them. These were women that had been given life sentences. As I

looked upon their faces I was in awe at the outer beauty of these women. These were women who made bad choices in life. I thought to myself that these women were somebody's daughter, mother, sister, aunt, cousin and friend.

As they began the play called FACES, I was both moved and touched by the testimonies of these women. Their objective is to turn a negative experience into something positive. If they could change one life it would give meaning to their own. They have no way of going on the outside, so we have to go inside to them. I do know that many people say that they don't like going into a prison setting. I say to that I don't believe that there is anyone in their right frame of mind who would say that they like prison or want to be there. All too often we as Christians think that we are exempt from falling prey to the tactics of the enemy. As it was stated in the play, you don't have to do anything except be in the wrong company at the wrong time. It is nothing like seeing and hearing about it first hand. We even had the opportunity to interact with the women at the end.

I wanted to know if this could be something presented to the church in the near future. It is for the young (middle school and high school) as well as the old who may be interested.

From a former inmate:

I have been to the institution to meet with I–WISH several times, and have had the opportunity to view FACES on two separate occasions. The first time I viewed the play, it was an emotional experience, so much so that I invited several friends and associates to attend one of its

viewings. One, a long time friend and professor…
brought three judges with her. They were so
impressed that a project to document the play
using paraprofessional student actors (was
discussed).
… I do not and will not align myself with
anything or anyone that is not positive and
constructive. This group of women deserves all
the consideration allowed to continue with this
worthy project.

From a college professor:

I was deeply impressed and moved by the play
when I was fortunate enough to see it in June. I
have worked with prison writers both locally and
nationally for decades in the well–rewarded belief
that sustained, continuous creative work like the
work that went into this play can go far to help
both inmates and others (making good use of
their time; modeling wise choices by people who
are incarcerated; making better choices by those
who are not). As an in–house tool, the play is
tremendously valuable. The members of I–WISH
have come up with something immensely valuable.
Betty May, the actor/teacher/director who worked
with the I–Wish members, providing cohesion
among the writing the women produced, creating
the performance–version of the play, and
directing its production, has done something
amazing. She has brought together hopeless
women and given them hope, a reason to live, if
only as better and more valuable citizens of
prison. I was stunned by the play, and even more
stunned by talking with some of the inmate actors
afterwards, there in the gym. Their lives have
suddenly become productive—and I don't just

mean productive to themselves. I mean to people in general, starting with their fellow inmates.

I worked for decades with lifers at [a men's prison], "going in" week after week for years to work with the Writers' Club, and it was easy to see how these men grew to be excellent mentors to younger men coming into [the prison]. They were respected by both inmates and authorities. Without them, the violence at [the prison] might have been even greater. And it overjoys me that the ex–inmate writers of several books, which my off–campus publishing company has brought out, are all legally free and prospering. Why? The answer is clear: because of the respect, knowledge, and creative possibilities [that] the [prison's] Writers' Club afforded them

It is only right—and wise—to maintain this kind of opportunity for women.

From a reporter:

I have not seen the play, but have heard multiple praises for its effective portrayals of regret, reconciliation and redemption by those who have committed crimes.

In my years as a reporter covering the legislature, Congress, police, crime and the courts, I have seen how a program like this can change the future of a person's life.

Seeing a way out of the jungle is building a future for a person. Not knowing how to get there is frightening. This program tells them how to start doing it.

Giving an inmate a little self–esteem for spelling out her redemption gives her a step up to the door outside.

From a retired chaplain:

I saw the play FACES and it touched me deeply.
The women were professional and spoke from
their hearts. As a former prison chaplain, the play
helped me to get a deeper understanding of what
had led women, women just like me, down a
wrong path. I am anxious that the play resume so
that I can invite girls at risk from some of our
services to the poor as well as our central office
staff members who are involved in planning
services for the poor and others.
I think the women can do a great service to the
community through this play. Knowing that they
are helping others is valuable for them as well.
They are part of our community although a wall
separates them from us. We are all God's children
and we are called to help one another.

From a church member:

I am writing to you because I have seen the play
FACES and enjoyed it from the time they started
until it ended. As I listened to each lady, they filled
my heart with such joy and love for the women
they have become, and how God has healed their
minds and hearts and given them the growth to
become better women. When they spoke, you
could tell they were free from that deep hurt,
anger, fear and all the other things that happened
in their lifetime. The performances will help the
young teens and elderly take action on their lives,
before they end up in prison, or dead or other.

From a reader:

I am moved to my core by [the women's] honesty, love, sadness, hope, despair and all of the emotions that define our humanity. Do they speak their own stories? Or are they speaking all stories of so many broken people?

Clarinda's letter to the jury: strong, true, crying for real justice in an unjust world. Clarinda's poem/letter to God: integrated whole of consistency that flies in the face of "good society's" judgment!

Jayna moves me to tears. What truth! What sorrow! What a powerful woman who can live with what is unbearable pain.

OMG, my heart BREAKS to read Danielle, Clarinda, Talia, Toni, et al. They portray their longings for freedom so powerfully. They portray the longings that unite us as brothers and sisters in this life. They look for the best. They experience many, many desolations that would cause most to succumb.

Tolanda's tormented anguish is the voice of a soul in hell. Ohhhh…groans of sympathy and sorrow for that soul that has to suffer so for the rest of her life. What a torment. It is demented that we consider this justice. What is?

Jayna tells of her aborted suicide and her hope to live—even in prison. I hope she finds life worth living.

Sheila writes so beautifully about the things those of us who are 'free' sometimes forget are so beautiful. Thank you, Sheila, for your beautiful heart.

Jayna, the prayer for the something missing. You found a beautiful part of yourself that is REAL and unending. People in the free world fail to find that. Stay with that. You are, your peace is, real. To each of you. To all of you. I am human, too.

You have touched me deeply with your honesty, your despair, your hope, your loss, your purpose, and your beautiful hearts. You asked us to forgive you. I forgive you. I really do. Will you please forgive me for being part of an unjust world—for paying for prisons—for not finding a better alternative?

I will pray for you each, every day.

I was blown away by FACES. I could barely endure the very intense stories of pain, betrayal, brokenness, and hope. [The] production NEEDS to be SEEN.

I hope you will pass along to your writers that I was deeply moved by their stories—each story. I wish for them a second chance. I know they wish that, too, and it is truly sad they may not get that chance. The chance they do have is the chance to tell their stories to people who will be impacted by their stories.

I wish I had a lot of money. You and I both know it would take more than the story to make a long–term difference in the lives of so many. So many of us, young people from deprived backgrounds especially, need a safe and caring relationship. I wish…

CHAPTER SIX:
The Kids

The women meet their targets

We had a second public performance the following night, and the audience reaction was the same. The women were thrilled, but they were anxious for the true test—the young people. Their mission remained the same: to reach out to at–risk kids and warn them about the consequences of bad choices. Their mantra still swam in their heads: *If we can help just one kid, all of our work will be worth it.* So, where were the kids?

The following week we had the answer: two groups of troubled girls, brought to the prison by their counselors and social workers. Their slumped walks through the hall, down the stairs, and into the gym told me they were definitely not happy about being there. The smell of tomato sauce permeated the air; I was glad it wasn't canned peas.

They flumped into the chairs, arms folded, eyes half closed, an attitude of "What kind of shit are they shoving down our throats now?" written all over their faces. Just the kids we were looking for. The women were in the dressing room and I rushed to tell them. They practically drooled at the thought of finally meeting the people for whom the show was intended.

At first, as the teenagers half listened to the women's stories of abuse, abandonment, and neglect, they hardly raised their heads. Then reactions started. Slowly. Eyes opened a little more, but arms still folded, bodies still slouched in their chairs, legs still outstretched. They were listening—barely. Then eyes opened a little wider, hands dropped into laps, backs straightened, feet flattened on the floor.

One by one they sat upright and slid to the edges of their seats. Some clasped their hands; others gripped the sides of their chairs. They were hearing their own stories. Stories they never told anyone. Stories they kept buried inside, eating their souls, filling them with shame and self–loathing. Many of the girls wept; one had her face buried in her counselor's shoulder.

The women hammered their message home:

You are not alone!
Abuse is not your fault!
Tell someone. If they don't believe you, tell someone else!
There is help!
There are people who care!
Stay in school!
Be a leader!
Stand up for yourself!
You are worth it!
Love yourself!
It may be too late for us. It is not too late for you!

The question–and–answer session was brief. It was obvious the girls just wanted to meet the women one–on–one. Mary Pat invited them to the stage and the women and the girls rushed into each others' arms, each comforting the other: sisters in a world the women had left behind, a world the girls were just beginning to experience, a world most of us will never understand.

"You are beautiful," the women told the girls.
"You are beautiful," the girls told the women.

We had several groups of girls come to see the play. The reaction was always the same. The girls left with hope in their hearts, knowing they were no longer alone, ready to accept the help they so desperately needed. The women watched them go with pride in their souls, wishing they could go with them, wishing they could protect them. As the girls filed out the gym door, one of the actors said, "If I had seen this play when I was a teenager, I probably wouldn't be here now."

And then the letters came. One girl decided to buckle down in school, earn good grades so she could work in the field of social justice. Another declared an interest in prison ministry. A fourteen–year–old went to work serving meals in a soup kitchen. The women wanted to save one child; here was documented proof they had saved three. And these are only the ones we know about. I'm sure many more took the women's words to heart.

What is the saying? "Save one child. Save the world." The women proved they could contribute to society even from behind bars. They may be faceless, invisible people, but their voices were heard. They made a difference. And they are proud.

From a youth group leader:

> I was privileged to take a group of ten young women (ages 15–17) and their mothers to [a performance of FACES]

> I will admit, I was a little nervous—and one of the teens that came along has not been the easiest child I've ever worked with. Driving to [the prison], she talked about how exciting prison life must be. The security process alone was enough to make her step back, and soon she was close by her mother's side as we slowly made our way into the gymnasium.

> The production was incredible and the girls (and their moms) were incredibly moved by what these

women have gone through, what they have lost and how they could make the world a better place by sharing their experiences. I knew the cast interacted with the audience at the end of the program, but wasn't sure how my kids would react. I was so proud of them!! They openly embraced and chatted with the cast, and the women were so nice to the girls—many of them telling the girls if they could save one woman from suffering their fate, then they had made a difference.

The play touched every member of our group – some who have never known anything less than a perfect childhood. The stories that bad things can happen to anyone—even in a perfect world—hit a nerve and touched their hearts. It was an amazing learning experience for the girls and their moms. We were all so glad we went! They keep asking when we can see it again!

We discussed the play for a few weeks. During Sunday School class, [the girls] shared our experiences with the United Methodist Women and in worship. The girls talked for weeks about FACES and **the child I was so worried about started volunteering in the church office and declared that she thought she would either like to get involved in social work or prison ministries!** Everyone who has heard about [FACES] has expressed interest in seeing [the play].

Not only do I work with teenagers at [my church], I am [a teacher].

[Our school] is involved in prison ministries. We have discussed the play and agree that having our students see it (all girls school, grades 9–12) would be an excellent learning opportunity.

I encourage the FACES program to continue. It is meaningful, informative, and shows that whether these women are clearly criminals, guilty because of a bad decision (theirs or the judicial system's), or completely innocent, they are human. They are courageous, paying for their mistakes and moving forward as best they can. My students still talk about the fact these women will never enjoy a dinner out or spend a day at the beach as long as they are in prison. The girls still talk about "earning" the privilege to have ice in their drinks.

Only by hearing it from the incarcerated women themselves does it have an impact on their young minds.

It was very hard to leave these amazing women and the girls asked if they could send them notes or gifts. We did send a letter congratulating them on a wonderful production but we have no idea if it was shared with them or not. This production is a great way to make a change in a positive way. The fact that many of these women were so very young when they were convicted makes it much more realistic to our teens.

I look forward to attending FACES again! (Can we arrange for boys to attend? I think it would be very beneficial for them to see how their actions can affect the lives of others!)

From a teacher:

A faculty member told me that she accompanied a group of teenage girls from her church to see FACES. **She shared how one of the young girls who attended the performance [had] been in** quite a bit of trouble herself, although not criminal activity. This young girl was profoundly moved by her experience of **FACES** and immediately changed the focus of her life and began to effectively and generously volunteer for service programs connected with the church and became goal oriented in her personal life.

From a mother:

My 16–year–old daughter and I attended FACES with our Youth Group. The performance was AMAZING and **had a powerful and very positive impact on my daughter.**
Hearing the stories of the inmates' reasons for incarceration and mistakes that they are having to live with was sad, but made a lasting impression on my daughter that I know will help her to avoid these bad decisions.
When the inmates came into the audience and talked to the girls about how important it is for them to stay in school and stay away from drugs, they REALLY connected with them.
My daughter still talks about the night and wants to go and visit with the inmates again. She says that it was a remarkable experience that she will remember all of her life. **It has led her to an interest in prison ministry.**

CHAPTER SEVEN:
The Population

Other inmates view the show

As with any society, the prison population has a hierarchy. I don't know who's on top, but lifers are certainly at the bottom. They are ridiculed and disrespected. Snide remarks are the norm:

"Oh. You're a member of I–WISH. Good name. You WISH you could go home someday. Too bad you never will."

It is a tough world and the women live it every day. There are those from the outside world who say: "So what? Serves them right. They made their choices." I understand the sentiment, but when you get to know the women as real people and not as the monsters depicted in the media, it is difficult to keep in mind the egregious crimes some of them committed.

The contempt the women experience is somewhat ironic. It is the lifers who do the most to help other inmates. They offer comfort to the newbies and often serve as mentors to the younger members of the population. They hold responsible positions in the institution, form committees, and present petitions of grievances or suggestions for making the prison as palatable an environment as possible.

In the beginning, there had been no doubt the members of I–WISH would perform the play for the population. It is common for groups of inmates to put together a show of some kind and present it to their peers. But this was different. In our play, the women presented their inner selves, revealing details about their lives that could be used as ammunition for more ridicule and derision.

When the date for the in–house performance was announced, the rumblings started slowly.

"I don't know about this. I don't want to give *them* anything more to talk about," one of the women said.

No doubt who the *them* were.

The group was divided. Some wanted to go through with it. "What do we care what *they* think?" Kilie said.

Others were afraid, fearing a future of sneers and jibes based on the secrets they would reveal: "I don't want *them* to know anything about me."

I don't know what more was said. Most of their discussions took place after hours; I only heard the aftermath. More and more it seemed the result would be: no show for the population. I didn't participate in the controversy; it was their decision, not mine. Finally, they took a vote. By a slim margin, the yesses carried the day—until the afternoon of the performance.

As usual, I got to the prison an hour or so before curtain. We finished positioning the chairs, detangling the sound system, and presetting the CD player. When everything was ready, I started the come–in music and left to find the cast. Our inmate audience was filing in—half the population, about four hundred people; the gym couldn't hold everyone. Audience members had to sign up to attend. Cast members told me the list filled up quickly.

On the way to meet with the performers, I glanced down at the gym through the hall windows. I could hear the music and the pre–show audience buzz I love so much. The inmates were not as intimidated by their surroundings as our public audiences had been.

I walked into the dressing room. It was silent. This was never the case. Once the original nervousness had passed, the women were always getting into their costumes, fixing their makeup, and chatting amongst themselves. This time they were gathered in small, frightened clusters. Even Kiley was having second thoughts about standing in front of the people she had to face every day of her life.

True, most of the inmates are not lifers. But there were still people with years to serve. And there were those who would be leaving and, perhaps, coming back. The entrances and exits to the prison are often revolving doors.

Some return to the world permanently. Would they repeat what they had heard in our play? Would the women's innermost secrets become juicy gossip to share at a crab fest? Wouldn't people on the outside just love to hear titillating details about perpetrators of crimes that had been headline news? Confinement may be a wretched way to live your life, but at least it offers privacy and relief from the media hounds.

And I know, as an actor, the most terrifying audience is the one that includes your family and friends. Like it or not, the women's fellow prisoners are their family. And their circle of friends—and enemies. They can never get away from them. Small towns are often rampant with gossip; this community of eight hundred women is no different.

I felt broken–hearted for them. These were some of the most courageous people I had ever met. Just getting though a day took more bravery than I had to generate in a year. I sat with them a while, unable to think of anything to say.

Finally I said, "It's your decision, but if you don't go on, they win."

After a few minutes about half of them stood, ready to face the crowd. But there was still the other half.

Then a note came from the warden's office. Brenda is too much of a lady and a professional to put it this way, but the essence of the message was: "Get your butts out there and do your thing." Smiles broke out. They knew their warden and they knew what the message meant: "I believe in you."

Everyone lined up, backs straight, ready for their entrance.

I returned to the gym and faded out the come–in music. The officers dimmed the lights, and the women paraded in, faces grim. If there were any snickers from the audience, I didn't hear them.

They started their lines, but did not make eye contact with audience members. They were looking at the walls, the ceiling, the speakers, and, worst of all, the floor. Anywhere but at the people in front of them. I moved to the back to give them someone to talk to.

I'm not sure when they realized their fellow inmates were listening, but slowly, one by one, the performers began talking to them, embracing them, entreating them to understand what they were trying to do. And the audience responded.

Laughter abounded at the references to prison life, especially during a brief re–enactment of a middle–of–the–night count. Heads nodded and tears flowed as they related the abuse they had suffered in their early years. The question–and–answer session was filled with expressions of gratitude and congratulations. Several of the younger inmates stood, thanked the performers, and said the play gave them courage to fulfill their sentences, get out of the prison, and stay out.

Choking back tears, one of them said it best: "Thank you. I swear, I'm going to get my GED, finish my sentence, and never come back here again." Or words to that effect. I don't remember the exact phrasing. By that time, I was pretty emotional myself.

It was what happened in the days following the performance that was the most gratifying. At the next I–WISH meeting, the women reported the inmates' responses.

"They wanted to know more," one of the cast members said. "They treated me with respect."

A young inmate had taken one of the actors aside and said, "I didn't know all you had been through. I'm sorry."

Still another member of the inmate audience said, "You told my story. Thank you."

The population has changed some since our last show, but those who remember the women's amazing performance still treat the lifers with the respect they deserve as fellow human beings. After two years, a new warden came in and cancelled the show citing security concerns and the workload on the staff. The women miss the play and their part in making the world a better place. They still make appeals to the administration to reconsider the decision.

Whatever happens, they stood up for themselves and they saved three lives. Perhaps many more. They fulfilled their mission and lived out their mantra. All the work was worth it.

CHAPTER EIGHT:
The Song is Ended

The Aftermath

Two years after the last performance, Mary Pat learned of a program sponsored by Prisons Foundation, an organization in Washington, D.C. that promotes the artwork and literary efforts of incarcerated men and women throughout the United States.[3] For the past few years, the Foundation had participated in The Kennedy Center for the Performing Arts' annual *Page to Stage Festival*, a public event that allows aspiring playwrights to showcase their work. Prisons Foundation had presented plays written by inmates under the title: *From Prison to Stage*.

I submitted FACES. They not only accepted the play, they asked me to compile and edit the script for the 2013 production and direct the show. I was thrilled for the women and for me. In the Baltimore/D.C. area, The Kennedy Center is our Broadway.

About twenty–five plays were published on the Foundation's website; I chose ten. Most were one–acts, although some were pages long. I edited the plays into formats that could be played on a bare stage and interspersed them with lines from FACES. Sometimes the editing was massive: one eighty–page play—complete with helicopters,

---

[3]prisonsfoundation.org.

airplanes, ships, and submarines—got reduced to one paragraph.

We had a good cast and the play was a huge success. The staff at The Kennedy Center's Family Theater couldn't have been more helpful and welcoming. I only wished the women of I–WISH could have been there. But they were ecstatic to have parts of their play performed outside the prison. They wanted their voices heard beyond the prison walls. We never dreamed their words would reach such a prestigious venue. The show was so successful I was invited back to write and direct the 2014 production.

This time, however, I didn't have FACES to fall back on. About twenty–five new plays were submitted, some wonderful—some not so wonderful. I needed more material. The Foundations' website also publishes poetry and fiction and nonfiction projects written by prison inmates. I read a hundred–plus books of poetry and scanned through more than two hundred fiction and nonfiction pieces. I chose four plays and interspersed them with incredibly beautiful poetry and prose. The process took six months, but I ended up with a script I thought—I hoped—would work.

In June we had auditions. Two of the actors from the previous year, Ed Higgins and Raoul Anderson, returned—a fact for which I was extremely grateful. They were joined by seven others: Lorena Berger, LaTasha Do'zia–Earley, Miriam Ferguson, Lauren Jackson, Jesse Milliner, Briana Ortiz, and John Raley. I list their names because this was a landmark occasion for me. In my entire career as performer, stage crew, and director, this was the only show in which I was involved that had no diva/os. Their talent and professionalism were outshone only by their willingness to work hard and by how much fun we had together during the rehearsal process. It was an honor to be part of this incredible company of theatrical professionals.

The script worked and, once again, the Kennedy Center staff was open and welcoming. The production was a rousing success: packed house—standing room only—and an enthusiastic response. It was even better than the year before. At the end of the show I reminded the audience that the flowing prose they had just witnessed was only a small sample of the minds we, as a society, are throwing away.

The women of I–WISH are proud of what they accomplished with FACES and they continue to offer their assistance to the prison and to the outside world.

- They serve as mentors to the younger inmates, give them a sympathetic shoulder to cry on, and help them adjust to prison life. I have no doubt they have prevented many mental breakdowns and suicides.
- They heard about a food bank in Baltimore City that was running low on supplies, so they gathered cans of food for poor families.
- A judge, the Honorable Brenda Murray, sponsored a Women's Reentry Program, designed to help prerelease inmates prepare for the outside world. Even though the program could not help them, the lifers took part in the planning and helped with the details, including modeling clothing in a fashion show of business attire.
- They wanted to do something for homeless children, so they created greeting cards with inspirational words of encouragement designated for the children's lunch bags.

They are involved with justice issues as well. In cooperation with the Maryland Crimes Victims Resource Center, they are planning a presentation to the entire prison population regarding the impact of crime on victims, and they are raising money for a donation to the Community Conferencing Center for Restorative Justice (Chapter Fifteen).

Attendance at the I–WISH meetings dropped off a bit after the play closed, but Mary Pat and Susan continued to bring in outside speakers and activities. At one point they asked me to conduct a creative writing class.

That was fun. I gave the women writing prompts and they came up with incredible material just as they had for the play. We discussed the elements of writing: use the senses, develop your characters, establish a story arc, and so on.

For an exercise of, "show don't tell," I gave the women a list of adverbs and adjectives and asked them to write a sentence that would show the word without saying the word. One of the words was: *short*. One woman wrote: "Betty came into the room, but I couldn't see her over the table." Cute. There's always a wise guy.

They wrote more about their lives and feelings and wonderful short stories they read aloud to each other. We experimented with poetry: rhythm, rhyme, sonnets, haiku, and freestyle. But without the play, without a goal, interest waned.

The holiday season approached—a time just as hectic in a prison as anywhere else. Red and green decorations cover the walls and hang from the ceiling and paper menorahs adorn the bulletin boards. There are parties in the cellblocks and small gatherings of the various volunteer groups. Christmas music blares from the cells and offices just as it does in the outside world. The inmates look forward to a special dinner—second only to the Thanksgiving spread.

The biggest celebration is the Family Christmas Party. The women asked me to don my clown persona and entertain. It sounded like fun and I looked forward to meeting the women's families.

Getting into the prison with all my equipment was not easy. Usually, when I attend meetings with the women, I only have the basics: notebook, pencils, pens, and perhaps a book or two. For the party I was loaded down with a large red duffel bag stuffed with magic tricks and juggling paraphernalia, a satchel full of balloons, a balloon pump, a ukulele, and a sheaf of sheet music. Everything had to be x-rayed, searched, and inspected. The gatehouse was crowded with partygoers, but they were patient while the officers went through my gear.

The only beings that had difficulty with my presence were the drug-sniffing dogs. I never knew dogs could look puzzled, but the smell of greasepaint confused them. They jutted their muzzles in and around my face and wig, looked up at their handlers with "What-the-hell-is-that-stuff?" looks in their eyes, and then went back to tickling my ears. A bit of pre–entertainment for the handlers, the officers, and the attendees.

A little boy, frightened by the crowd, the noise, and the uniformed officers, hid behind a trash receptacle and refused to go through the gigantic metal detector. I whipped out a long yellow balloon, blew it up, and twisted it into a flower.

I knelt and handed it to him. "Give this to your Mommy," I whispered. "It will make her happy."

He seized the flower with both hands and trotted through the machine, proud to have a gift for his mom.

The party took place in the prison gym—usually a gray/green venue devoid of any joy. Now it was transformed. Homemade red and green chain links looped around the room, and handcrafted poinsettias and holly sprigs bloomed in every corner. Hand printed signs papered the walls: *Merry Christmas, Happy New Year,* and a few wishing everyone a *Happy Hanukkah.*

The party was pretty much like any other holiday get–together. There were two hundred to three hundred people present. The kitchen staff provided a beautiful buffet lunch, and a group of young women presented a Christmas play and led the crowd in a medley of carols. And, of course, Santa made a visit with donated presents. I did a little show and made balloon animals for all the kids. It was fun and everyone had a good time.

Until it was time to leave.

About fifteen minutes before the scheduled closing, I spotted a little girl, three or four years old, sitting on an older girl's lap, sobbing. I approached her.

"Can I help?" I asked. "Did she hurt herself?"

"No," the older girl replied as she rocked her little sister. "I told her the party will be over soon and she doesn't want to leave Mommy."

I felt the sting of tears, but choked them back. Clowns don't cry. I felt helpless. I made her a balloon dog. I even made a leash for the dog. It didn't help.

When the time came for the visitors to leave, the officers lined them up at the gym door. They would be taken into a small room where they would wait until count had cleared and all the inmates had been checked for contraband—a humiliating experience that involves inspection of every body orifice. The women were separated and sent to the bleachers, where they sat and cried and waved to their loved ones.

The guests were on their way out when a little boy shouted, "Mommy! Mommy!" He broke from the crowd and ran to his mother. He threw his arms around her neck and wouldn't let go. An officer had to pry him out of her arms. The strained look on the officer's face told me she was as upset about the heartbreaking tears as everyone else. She carried the child to a woman I assumed to be the boy's grandmother. She clutched him to her and patted his back. The crowd filed out, the little boy's sobs still echoing in the gym.

I heard a child's voice. "Why is the clown crying?"

CHAPTER NINE:
The Women Behind the Faces

Who were they? Who are they now?

The age–old argument for keeping convicted murderers in jail is always in the air: "At least their families can visit them. The only place the victim's families can visit their loved one is the cemetery."

A valid argument. Even the women agree.

One of the women said to me, "If you and Mary Pat and Susan really knew what some of us have done, you'd never come back." I don't know whether or not she was referring to herself.

Yes, there are those in prison who should never see the other side of the walls, but most of the women with whom I work were in desperate circumstances from which they saw no way out, or they were kids, too immature to foresee the consequences of foolhardy decisions. They had no one in whom they could confide and didn't know anyone who would listen and help. Others were addicted to drugs or alcohol and under the effects of that disease. Still others acted out as the result of lifelong, undiagnosed, and untreated mental illness.

Each woman has a story, some so wretched it is beyond difficult to relate. No doubt they made the wrong choice; murder can never be the answer. But these stories must be told if we are ever to understand and help people overcome life circumstances that lead to tragedy.

Their stories speak of terrible abuse, first from fathers—and mothers—then from husbands. They are women who snapped after the fifth or fiftieth time they begged for help from an uncaring system—help that never came. There are young people, caught up in inner city crime, sentenced to life at age fifteen or sixteen. There are women who witnessed their children being abused, who killed to protect them. All of them live with their crimes, filled with remorse and guilt, always asking, "What if…?"

In FACES, Jayna expressed the emotions of many of the women I've met:

> Sometimes it's hard for me to look into a mirror. Yes, even after all these years, I still feel ashamed and even embarrassed. I cry from time to time because it still hurts really bad. And, I ask myself: why am I crying? I guess I still cry for myself and even for my family, especially my children. But, most important, I cry for my victims. Because in no shape, form, or fashion did "they" deserve any of this. And, the realization of it all makes my heart heavy. I become so sad and empty inside. Lots of times, I look around this place and I can't believe that I am here. I shake my head and close my eyes and always wonder: What if?

While most of the women come from unbearable circumstances and horrific backgrounds of emotional, physical, and sexual abuse, some fall into more mundane categories. Several are from lower and middle class families, rebellious kids looking for a better life. Translation: more stuff. They wanted everything they saw advertised on television and in the fashion magazines they devoured. They wanted the "good life"—fancy cars, expensive jewelry, designer clothing, and exotic travels.

Every day, kids just like the kids these women once were see the people who have the things they so fervently desire. On the way to one school in Prince Georges County, Maryland, the bus passes a well–known drug market. The parking lot is full of Cadillacs, Jaguars, and Mercedes Benzes. The drug dealers, pimps, and prostitutes wear fancy clothes and drape themselves with gold and silver "bling." The formula is simple: fancy cars + expensive jewelry + designer clothes = success. As one of the cast members in FACES put it, "… the amount of money you can make in a week working a nine to five job, I can make in a day hustling."

Then the kids get to school. The teachers' parking lot is full of Chevys and Volkswagens; the teachers wear clothes they get on sale at JCPenney or Sears. The choice is obvious. All the talk about "feeling good about yourself," "helping others," or "making a difference in the world" is, to them, the *whomp–whomp–whomp* sound effect of a loser.

Some of the women are incarcerated because of gang activity. Often women receive longer sentences because of a misplaced loyalty to other gang members—particularly boyfriends. Then they find the sleazy boyfriends aren't quite as loyal to them. A prosecutor will often offer a plea bargain[4] to the first person who confesses or turns state's evidence.[5]

---

[4] A plea deal is a negotiation between the defendant and his attorney on one side and the prosecutor on the other, in which the defendant agrees to plead "guilty" or "no contest" to some crimes, in return for reduction of the severity of the charges, dismissal of some of the charges, the prosecutor's willingness to recommend a particular sentence, or some other benefit to the defendant. Sometimes one element of the bargain is that the defendant reveal information such as location of stolen goods, names of others participating in the crime, or admission of other crimes. http://legal–dictionary.thefreedictionary.com.

[5] A person accused of a crime "turns state's evidence" when he or she decides to give the prosecutor evidence about the crime, including facts about other participants in the crime (or other crimes) in return for lenient treatment, a plea bargain, and/or a recommendation of a light sentence. *Ibid.*

Sometimes the boyfriends place the blame on their girlfriends and receive lighter sentences. As young girls they are too young and immature to understand the need to look out for themselves and the consequences of their silence.

Sometimes the boys over eighteen convince the underage girls to take the blame for a crime. "You're a minor. All you'll get is a little time in juvy." They feed them the details and the girls confess. The girls end up in adult court and sentenced to life in prison.

Another result of gang activity is the pressure the men lay on the women to prostitute themselves to earn money for them, an endeavor that often results in violence. One woman said, "He told me if I loved him I would do it." Sometimes this leads to the horror of sex–based human trafficking as well (Chapter Twelve).

A few of the inmates are from the more privileged classes. They grew up with everything and felt they were entitled to more. I recognized the type from my experience as a high school teacher: indulged kids who know everything and can't be bothered to listen or pay attention to a lowly, underpaid teacher—the kind of student whose one–day absence can make a teacher feel like he or she has been granted an additional week of life. If that sounds harsh, chances are you've never been a high school teacher.

Most of these kids turn out fine. In fact, they often return after graduation to apologize for their behavior. Some of them actually go on to be teachers—karma working in the very best way. For a few, however, their desire for the "good life," and their feelings of entitlement spiral out of control, and violence isn't far behind.

The one thing every lifer I've met has in common, no matter her station in life, is low self–esteem and feelings of worthlessness. Over and over I heard the same things: "I didn't like myself." "I thought I was stupid." "I was ugly." "I was too fat." "I was too skinny." "My mother told me I ruined her life." "My father left because I'm no good." And their adolescent minds came up with the same remedy: boys. They turned to sex, equating intimate physical relations with love.

It is ironic that landing in prison gives them what they always needed: medical and psychological treatment, compassion, and understanding. Through treatment programs and therapy, the women come to terms with themselves and their pasts. They learn why they did the things they did. They learn to like—even love—themselves. They become the women they were meant to be, even if it is too late for them to have a "normal" life. The point is this: ***They are not the same people they were when they committed their crimes.***

Many of the women have worked hard to earn a second chance at life and are deserving of that opportunity. They have gone through therapy, taken anger–management classes, and worked to earn GED and AA degrees. Often it is society that failed them in the first place. We cannot fail them again.

In discussing their stories, I am not going to dwell on their crimes —rather on who they were before the tragic events and who they are now. Suffice it to say, they have all been accused, tried, and convicted of capital offenses and sentenced to life in prison. In all but one case, their victims are dead.

KRISTA

Krista never misses an I–WISH meeting. Every time I see her I figuratively slap my head. My first thought is always: *What the hell is she doing here?*

She is intelligent—make that brilliant. She is well educated. She carries herself with pride. In a dispute, she is always the first one to offer a reasonable solution. She is well read; she recommended one of the books in my bibliography. She writes beautifully. She's loving and compassionate toward the other inmates. She's a leader in the prison, does well in school, and performs her job as clerk in the sewing shop with competence and professionalism. She's gorgeous, well groomed, and neatly coiffed.

I repeat: *What the hell is she doing here?*

"I was raised by my grandmother," Krista told me. "She died when I was seven—left a big hole in my life. But I did well in school—straight A's. I loved reading the most. I always had a book in my hand.

"When I was twelve I got raped."

She stopped talking for a moment, almost as if she were reliving the event.

"The man raped my soul. I didn't tell anyone except my best friend, but she told my mother. Mom blamed me and shamed me. I turned in. I got defiant and I lost all interest in school. Started getting Ds and Fs.

"By the time I turned thirteen I was shy and lonely. I had no friends and nobody to talk to. I tried to please people. I did anything I could so people would like me. Then I found out boys liked me if I had sex with them.

"When I was fifteen my father remarried. I didn't get along with my stepmother. She hated me. So I ran away. I thought if I weren't there maybe people wouldn't fight so much. It didn't help. I started drinking and going to clubs. Some people there tried to talk me into taking money for sex.

"By eleventh grade I was an unhealthy, dysfunctional person. I couldn't think for myself and I had no hopes for a future. When I was seventeen I had my son.

"When I was twenty I met three guys—not nice people. And that's when everything happened.

"I was in the car when the three of them jumped out. They robbed two men and shot them dead. I wasn't involved in the murder. I didn't even know they had guns. I heard the shots, and then they jumped back into the car and put a gun to my head and said if I told anyone about what went down they would kill me, my son, and my whole family.

"My lawyer called me a 'nonparticipant,' but because I was there I was convicted of first–degree murder and sentenced to life without parole.

"My son is now twenty–six. My father raised him. I'm forty–four. My father and I came to grips with each other. We share a beautiful relationship. We're best friends. My dad and my son are still fighting for me and they're working on another appeal.

"I've taken advantage of every therapeutic and educational opportunity [the prison] offers. Now I can think for myself. I'm the best person I know. I will never again allow anyone to think for me."

She stopped talking for a while, alternately staring at the table and gazing at the ceiling. I waited.

"I dream of being free. Someday. Maybe. I want to be with my father and my son. I would love to run a business. Maybe someday own my own home."

Krista's conviction is a prime example of the outrageous effects of the Felony Murder Law (Chapter Fourteen). A few months ago she had a post conviction hearing. A week later her lawyer called with exciting news: her sentence had been changed from life without parole to life with parole. When Mary Pat, Susan, and I got to the prison she couldn't wait to tell us about it.

"I'll be out by Christmas!" she said.

But two months later, when she returned to court, the news was far from exciting. "The judge told me to come back in three years. He said we'd talk about it then."

Krista took a few days to cry and feel sorry for herself. Then she went back to work helping other inmates and working on improving conditions in the prison. She took part in this year's "Reentry Conference," a two–day program sponsored by the Women's Reentry Program that offers assistance and advice for women eligible for release. She modeled business attire in the fashion show and walked the runway with style and elegance.

THEA

The one word that comes to mind when I think of Thea is:

"sweet." Blond and blue–eyed, it is obvious she had been a beautiful young woman. Now she is missing a few teeth, gray strands overpower her once ash–blond hair, and her eyes are dull with the pain of disappointment.

She is a gentle woman who doesn't say much, but has much to offer when she does speak up. She was too shy to perform in FACES, but she was always in the background, assisting in any way she could. She helped set up the gym and she served as a side coach, ready to prompt anyone who got stuck on a line or remind an inattentive actress of a missed cue.

It was difficult for her, but she managed to tell me her story.

"I grew up on Maryland's Eastern Shore. I have four big brothers. I loved my brothers. All I ever wanted was to fit in with them. Have them accept me. I wanted to play with them. I wanted them to like me, to accept me. I would have done anything to make my family happy. But they hit me and they did sex things to me.

"When I was thirteen my parents got divorced and I moved back and forth between them. I was the only girl and I was the only one who went back and forth so I got away with a lot. They let me go almost anywhere and do anything I wanted to do. In high school I hung out with the 'in' crowd and fooled around with liquor and drugs.

"After high school I had a couple of jobs, but I always wanted to join the Peace Corps. When I was twenty–one I went to Washington, D.C. to apply, but when I got there I found out I was pregnant. I went back home, got married, and had two more kids."

She stood up suddenly. "I got to go." She called for an officer to let her into the restroom. She returned a few minutes later, eyes red.

"After that, everything went bad. My mom was in an accident and got crippled. I had to take care of her and my husband and kids. Then my husband started running around.

Then my mom died. I blamed myself for everything and had a nervous breakdown.

"Then I was in a car accident—got hurt really bad. I was in so much pain. They operated on my back twice, but it didn't help. So I started drinking.

"One night, I was at a friend's house. I got really drunk. There was a fire and my friend died. We were fighting before the fire so everyone said I did it. No one ever figured out how the fire started. All I know is I didn't start it.

"I was one kind of a person then. And today, I'm a different kind of person. I was a straight–up mess back then. I was dazed and confused. With very little self–worth or esteem. I had almost no hope and I had pretty much given up.

"The one thing I did still have that gave me a purpose in life was the love of my three wonderful children. They truly are everything to me. If not for having them I'm quite certain that I couldn't have lasted this long in here. However, I knew that I had put them through more than enough.

"All I can do is turn inside myself to the place in my heart that wants so desperately to feel human, and yet I just feel so empty. Whenever I'm having a pity party and feel worthless and about to give up, another inmate will ask me to write a letter for them, or draw a picture, or sew something, or fix something. And I'll say, 'Sure,' grateful to her for giving me another reason to be at peace within myself and stay connected to this world as if I have a purpose.

"Today, the woman that I am is clean, both physically and spiritually. I have remembered how to hold my head up, and speak without biting my tongue. And I do have the faith and hope that someday I will be released from here and become a productive member of society."

She looked up at me, and for a moment her blue eyes sparkled.

"Miracles don't happen on man's time. They happen on God's time."

DANIELLE

Of all the egregious applications of the Felony Murder Law (Chapter Fourteen), Danielle's case is one of the worst.

Danielle is a beautiful person inside and out. She is tall, elegant, and always beautifully groomed. In a just world she would be on the cover of *Ebony* magazine.

Her story is as heartbreaking as it is unbelievable.

"My parents had eight children and we were a happy family. My mother is a teacher. My father was a head foreman at Bethlehem Steel. He's dead now.

"We loved and trusted each other and we took care of each other. But it turned out all the trust I had in everybody was a big mistake. When I was fourteen my parents got a divorce and everything went wrong for my family and for me.

"I stuck it out as long as I could. Then, in eleventh grade, I got pregnant and dropped out of school. I married the father and had four more children by him. Ten years later he got involved with drugs and the marriage fell apart.

"I met a private investigator from Virginia. I was pregnant with his child when everything happened. The baby was born here. His father raised him. He's eighteen now and he's doing well.

"I had plans for my life. Two sisters, an uncle, and a cousin are Maryland State Troopers. I wanted to join, too. I was studying law enforcement—getting ready to apply to the academy. The man who attacked me and the judicial system destroyed any hopes for that.

Danielle told me about the event that changed her life. "The night of the crime, I was four months pregnant. I was home watching basketball on television when a family friend tried to rape me. I told my uncle, who told an ex–boyfriend, who went to the man's apartment and killed him. I was in the street outside the apartment. I didn't know what my ex meant to do. Someone saw me pointing at the rapist's window. I was arrested and charged as an accomplice. Under the Felony Murder Law, I was considered to be as culpable as my ex and I was sentenced to life in prison without parole. My ex–boyfriend was also given a life sentence. He died in prison.

"So here I am. Locked away from my children. One of them was gunned down in a drive–by shooting. They had to tell me about it over the telephone. I never got a chance to say good–bye or hold him one last time."

She left the room, unable to go on. On my next visit to the prison she told me more about the woman she is now and what she has been doing in the eighteen years of her incarceration.

"I am the same person now I was then, but my train of thought has matured. I've participated in the Women's Intense Treatment Program. I discovered my choices were the result of trusting too much."

Getting to know Danielle has been a privilege and a delight. She has an aura of peacefulness that is contagious. She is also, I believe, a born poet and actress. The lyrical imagery she wrote for FACES produced one of the most poignant moments in the play, and her delivery was impeccable:

> Sometimes I picture my life as a documentary. The
> wind starts to blow as a scene of an empty street
> is shown. A sanitation worker is sweeping up
> leaves and putting them into a trashcan.
> Everything goes into black and white, and then a
> judge's gavel comes down hard, hits the block, and
> a cell gate shows up in a flash and slams shut. The
> scene goes back to the trashcan and leaves start to
> blow up out of the can. Our faces are in the midst
> of the leaves, swirling around, trying to be free,
> but being pushed back into the trashcan.

Danielle continues to participate in the service dog program. She has trained six dogs. Lawyers are working on her case and they are optimistic. When she is released, she hopes to establish a business to train and groom dogs.

BRANDY

Brandy is a gorgeous, educated enigma. She is one of nine children from a loving, supportive, deeply religious family. An honor student in high school, she went on to college and was graduated with degrees in sociology and psychology. The murder for which she was convicted made headline news for months and several books have been written about the case. At first, she tried to lie her way out of it by making outrageous claims of an alleged break–in and rape, causing endless investigation and embarrassment for authorities.

She was tried, convicted and, despite numerous supportive letters from family and friends, sentenced to life in prison without possibility of parole. The victim's father pressed for the sentence. Devastated by the loss of his daughter, he didn't want to have to face Brandy in parole hearings. The judge agreed. The father's feelings are certainly understandable. The murder was gruesome and it was obvious the victim had suffered.

But what about thirty years from now? Or forty? What good does it do society to keep Brandy in jail for a crime— heinous though it was— she committed at age twenty–nine? Is it punishment or is it revenge?

This is one of the questions that keeps me tossing and turning at night. Would the death penalty be kinder? I cannot accept that. On an executed criminal's death certificate, the cause of death is often listed as "Homicide." If my taxes contribute to his or her execution, does it follow I am guilty of felony murder?

TONI

The only child of a teenage mother, Toni showed a streak of rebelliousness right from the start. She is from Washington, D.C., where her mother was a District of Columbia police officer. Toni grew up in a turbulent household. Married at age fourteen, Toni's mother divorced her first husband as well as her second.

"I rebelled," Toni told me. "Got into a lot of trouble. I wanted to hurt my mother because of her marriage to my stepfather. I didn't get along with him and I started drinking.

"When I was twelve I went to live with my uncle and I hated my stepfather even more because I was away from my mother. I had violent thoughts about him. I wanted to kill him. It made me afraid. I thought maybe I had the mind of a killer.

"I began shoplifting in stores, which embarrassed my whole family. At fourteen everybody in the juvenile judicial system knew me and I had served time in juvy.

"By high school, I was a full–blown alcoholic. I used PCP and cocaine, too. I was the school's party girl. I loved designer clothes. They called me 'Polo' because I especially liked the Ralph Lauren line. I got the clothes any way I could.

"When I was seventeen and a half, I met a man who moved me into a condo. For eleven years I stayed at home, high on PCP. I had two kids.

"After we broke up, I met and married a Washington, D.C. police officer. I stopped doing drugs and cleaned myself up. I had two more kids and went to work for a cable company, installing telephone and television cable services all through Maryland. On weekends, I worked at a second job— unarmed security. It was a good life. We had everything we needed. We even traveled a lot."

She didn't want to talk about her crime and I didn't press the issue. All I understood was: everything was great until violence ended it.

"In prison I have learned not to sweat the small stuff. I've taken anger–management classes and participated in other activities that might help my chance for parole. But I'm always depressed. I'm just tired of waking up in the morning.

"My children are grown now. My oldest turned to drugs and alcohol after I was locked up, but he's working as a massage therapist now. One of my boys is on his way to a degree in chemical engineering and another joined the army.

My youngest, a daughter, is in college studying physical therapy.

"My husband and I never really divorced. I hope someday we can get together again. My mom died last year. That's my biggest regret. I know I let her down.

"I'm studying to be an evangelist in the Church of Redeemer Bible Institute. And I hope someday I can go home and make up for all the time I lost with my children."

JAYNA

"My mother was fourteen years old when I was born. She never forgave me for surviving the abortion procedure she did to get rid of me. She reminded me about that every day of my life. I spent my childhood feeling guilty at being born and ruining my mother's life."

Jayna killed a man when she found him performing fellatio on her four–year–old son. "I do it all the time," the man said. "He likes it." In FACES, she recalled the moment:

> Something triggered in me when I walked in and saw the man molesting my son. At that moment I killed everything negative in my life. I killed my mother who didn't want me—pushing me to the side like some beat–up rag doll; the father who beat the crap out of my mother in front of me; the boyfriend who battered me; and the man who put a knife to my throat and raped me.

Unfortunately, she left the room to get the murder weapon. Under Maryland law, as in many other states, this means premeditation, and premeditation means a life sentence. She has been in prison for over forty years.

Compare this to the famous Scarsdale murder in the state of New York.[6] In 1980 Jean Harris went to Dr. Herman Tarnower's home gun in hand and shot him four times. She

---

[6] *Very Much a Lady: The Untold Story of Jean Harris and Dr. Herman Tarnower.* By Shana Alexander. New York: Little Brown & Co. 1983.

was sentenced to fifteen years to life and released eleven years after her conviction.

Jean Harris was from an affluent family. She was well educated and held a prestigious position at an elite girls' school. And she was white.

Jayna was from the inner city. She had limited education and few skills. And she is black.

Jean Harris had a battery of expensive lawyers.

Jayna had an overworked public defender.

Warden Brenda Shell–Eleazer had known Jayna for years. She never knew about the abuse Jayna had suffered until she saw FACES. That information was not in Jayna's record or in the trial transcript.

I asked Jayna why. "My mother wouldn't let me talk about it. She didn't want people to know the family's dirty laundry."

I don't think it's a coincidence that witnessing her son's abuse triggered Jayna's rage. I also don't think it's a coincidence that the then four–year–old is now a grown man, incarcerated, serving a life sentence of his own.

I talked to a lawyer who is working on Jayna's case. She said, "That's the way the law worked then. If it happened today, she'd be out in three or four years." Not much help for Jayna.

In 1993, Jayna was one of the lifers caught up in the "round–up" described in Chapter Fourteen. A state police car pulled up in front of the convenience store where she was working as a clerk. The officers marched through the door, put her in handcuffs and leg chains, pushed her into the cruiser, and drove her back to the prison. She was never allowed outside the walls again.

But somehow she has found peace. "I've learned to control my rage. And I've learned to love myself."

In FACES, she described her epiphany:

> Here, in prison, I worked hard at my job and I had
> therapy. I studied and earned my GED, but I had
> to find something bigger than me. It's something
> that when you get into trouble, or drink too much,

or when someone you love dies and you don't know what to do, you cry out for help, hoping that "something" is listening and has an answer. A part that seems to have no face or mouth or eyes, but you know it exists. "Something" bigger than me. As tears streamed down my cheeks and face, tremendous warmth overwhelmed me. My hands went up towards the sky. I fell on my knees not knowing why. However, there I was, trembling, head–bowed, submitting to what I believed to be that "missing piece." I was engulfed with solace. Quietness. An overwhelming sensation of completeness. I understood the missing piece. I found that "something" bigger than me.
I found the Good in me and I love her. I love her fiercely!

A year ago Jayna was transferred to another prison and we've lost touch. I miss her.

KILEY

Kiley's story has been told many times in newspaper and magazine articles and on television. Her case was a featured episode on the television series, *Snapped*. It is of particular interest because of the bizarre events surrounding the crime. I will not describe the event because the details would reveal Kiley's identity.

Kiley maintains her innocence and her family is behind her. They have launched a web site seeking support for a new trial.

Kiley was a skilled professional, respected in her field. To outsiders her family appeared to be the perfect unit: lovely wife, handsome husband, beautiful little daughter. What they didn't know was the agony Kiley was suffering at the hands of that husband. And they didn't know the sexual abuse she had suffered throughout her childhood at the hands of her stepfather. For years, she told no one about a situation that filled her with shame and self–loathing. In FACES, she tells about the day she finally confided in her mother:

> My mother chose him.
>
> Something inside my soul died, but I didn't cry; I kept right on preparing for my first prom. Lionel Ritchie and Michael Jackson play in a gymatorium filled with streamers and paper decorations. As we dance, I stare at the other teenagers. I marvel at their beauty, absolutely certain that every one of them is lucky, if only because they aren't me.
> I am her final sacrifice. I am a teenager and I have just learned my worth.

Kiley is a leader in the prison. She heads grievance committees and often speaks on behalf of people who have been accused of infractions. She teaches Pilates and offers advice on health and fitness. Her maturity and education stand out and make her a go–to person for other inmates when they need consolation. She takes part in creative writing courses and enrolls in every college class she can. She is a voracious reader and writer and refuses to let her mind rot in a place where that is all too possible.

ETHEL

Ethel's story is yet another example of the egregious effects of the Felony Murder Law (Chapter Fourteen).

"When I was nineteen I lived in Baltimore. I was walking with my boyfriend and we passed a friend's house.

"'Go knock on that door,'" he said.

"Why?' I asked.

"'Because he's mad at me and he won't answer the door for me.'

"I knocked on the door. They got into a fight and my boyfriend killed him."

At this point in the story she broke down. "I didn't do it. I swear I didn't do it. No one will believe me. I didn't do anything. I didn't know. I didn't. I didn't." She covered her face and sobbed. I embraced her, trying, but not succeeding, to offer comfort.

Ethel was sentenced to life. She has been in prison for over forty years.

I'm not so naïve that I don't know some of the women tell me what they want me to believe. But not Ethel. She is one of the sweetest, most compassionate people I have ever met. So many times, in rehearsal or just passing in the hall, I would see her deep in conversation with another inmate. Ethel was always the one listening, giving some desperate soul a shoulder to cry on.

I so enjoyed Ethel's presence all through the play process. Her supportive smile when the divas were giving me a hard time sometimes got me through the day. I always enjoyed her sense of humor and state of grace when she delivered one of her speeches in FACES:

> Sometimes, I lie down in the grass and look up at the sky and see different animal shapes in the clouds. That is cute and funny.
> Sky is beautiful. I wonder sometimes if, when I'm looking up at the sky, someone else in a different place is looking up at the sky, too?

Eleven years ago, after the years–long "risk–assessment" examinations required by The Parole Board Commission, the Board granted Ethel parole. Under Maryland law, the Governor's signature is required for any lifer before parole can go into effect. The Governor ignored Ethel's petition; it sat on his desk for years. Under a new law, the Governor has 180 days to sign (Chapter Fourteen). If he does not sign the petition, the parole goes into effect. The Governor denied Ethel's petition.

Ethel changed. She stopped coming to I–WISH meetings and, unless I happened to run into her on my way into the building, I rarely saw her. When I did see her, she was not the same smiling person she had been. The Governor's denial hit her hard and her depression was complete. She lost weight and she stopped talking. My heart broke for her.

Ethel once wrote: "Audacious hopes prevail in truth. Success begins now!" That person with the positive outlook was gone.

But, for once, there is a happy ending. In August 2013, Ethel was released under the Unger Ruling, a challenge that questioned the Constitutionality of instructions given to Maryland juries before 1980.[7] Susan and I went to her hearing in a Baltimore court. It was a wonderful, sunshiny day.

CLARINDA

Clarinda has been in prison for over thirty years. She practically runs the place. She is a lively five–foot bundle of

---

[7]In 1975 Merle W. Unger Jr. was tried and convicted for shooting and killing a police officer. At his trial, the judge told jurors that his instructions about the law were "merely advisory." At the appeal, the court ruled that those instructions would have allowed the jury to disregard Unger's rights — to find him guilty without proof beyond a reasonable doubt and ignore the presumption of innocence. This led to a 2012 Maryland Court of Appeals decision that is forcing prosecutors to revisit decades–old cases, mostly murders and rapes. Rather than risk an acquittal on retrial — fading memories of witnesses and lost evidence would make it difficult to take the cases before a jury — prosecutors in some of the earlier cases have negotiated deals that allow felons to be released on probation. Of those released, Brian M. Saccenti, the chief attorney for the appellate division of the Maryland Office of the Public Defender, said many of them have worked behind bars to better themselves. "All of the people we have represented who have been released are people who have done a lot of very positive things while incarcerated. In many cases, they have become really good men." —From: *Md. releasing some felons early after state high court ruling* By Lynh Bui and Dan Morse. *The Washington Post.* August 27, 2013. Jennifer Jenkins contributed to the report.

energy who has her fingers into every pie—busy, busy, busy. She works in one of the offices and knows everything that goes on in the prison. The administrators rely on her; they know if they give Clarinda a job it will get done. Although she is no longer a member of I–WISH, for years she never missed a meeting and her contributions were invaluable.

"I come from an extremely wealthy background. I am a descendant of the Wright brothers and grew up in high society, complete with expensive cars and designer clothes. Behind those doors, though, there was another world, a world of physical, emotional, and sexual abuse. I didn't tell anyone. I never cried. Crying brought more beatings.

"I was graduated from college with three degrees and I was highly respected in my professional life. I got married and looked forward to a life away from abuse. I didn't know I had married still another abuser. I suffered more years of physical torture and control. I begged for help from the 'system,' but no help came.

"I was accused and convicted of conspiracy to murder my husband. There may have been a conspiracy, but it wasn't mine and it didn't work. My husband is still very much alive. Another family member was the true conspirator."

Under the law in many states, including Maryland, conspiracy to murder means a life sentence, whether or not it is successful.

Clarinda continues to maintain her innocence and fight for exoneration. "My lawyer believes me and he is seeking a new trial."

Clarinda is in the same position as Ethel is: parole granted, then delayed, and finally denied by the Governor. She is almost seventy years old now. The years drag on with no resolution. But she never gives up. She carries a see–through portfolio bulging with papers and letters she is writing to secure her release. Somehow, she remains cheerful and upbeat. I don't know how she does it.

Clarinda was one of the few who had had experience on stage. Her impassioned plea for help for women suffering domestic abuse was a dramatic highlight in FACES:

> You ask why I didn't leave? Instead, ask the police why they were not there, or better yet ask my husband why he beat me. Question the prosecutors. Ask them why my husband was not imprisoned when he broke my bones. Put the judge in that same chair. Ask why the law was not upheld and punishment meted out before my husband beat me that last time.
>
> Look into yourself and ask how you can stop the abuse, and, when you return to that room to cast your vote, judge me NOT from the comfort of your life, but from the agony and terror of mine. Take with you what you heard while in the juror's box. Look at yourself and your neighbors. Face your responsibility in this tragic event and do your share that there be an end to lives lived as mine

"When I am released I want to work with women suffering from domestic violence. And I want to become an activist in the fight for fairness in the judicial system for victims of abuse."

SHANNA

Shanna, our designated spot operator, is a character. I absolutely adore her. She can be moody. Some days she laughs and smiles and fools around, and the next day she is morose and just wants to be left alone. I can usually gauge her mood by her walk.

"I have been in prison since I was in tenth grade," she told me. "I can't believe the judge sentenced me to life. I know I should serve time. But my whole life? I was fifteen years old. I was a stupid wild know–it–all kid. I didn't even think about what we were doing. I didn't believe anyone would really die.

"My boyfriend was in a gang so I joined, too. Besides that, you feel safe in a gang. It's like a family. They protect you. Baltimore is a tough town. Especially if you're black."

But the security of a gang comes at a price. In FACES, Sally described her feelings about gang life:

> In my senior year I joined a gang and the gang became my family. I felt safe. What I didn't know was that I wasn't really safe at all. Because when you're in a gang, you are the target of all the other gangs just because you are in your gang. Still, it is easier to follow; it is dangerous and scary to lead.

Shanna talked about the terrible day that transformed her life. "The girl broke one of the gang rules so we had to punish her. 'Set an example,' my boyfriend told me. We all went to the woods and then she was dead. It was all so stupid—I know that now. It could have been the other way around. If I had broken the rules, I would have been punished, too.

"One of guys with turned state's evidence. He's out of jail now. The other got life. I had no information, nothing to trade, so I got life without parole. And besides, I was a girl. The judges always go harder on girls."

I asked her to tell me about her life before the boyfriend, before the gang.

"In high school, I was a good student. As and Bs. I wanted to go to college. I wanted to be a psychiatrist."

She paused to take a long drink of water, and then rolled the paper cup in her hands. "I'm in my thirties now. I've earned my GED and I'm working on my Associate Arts degree with the Goucher College program in here. Maybe someday I'll get out. I want to help kids—maybe keep them from doing what I did. I try to keep on hoping, but it's hard. I pray a lot."

The 2012 Supreme Court ruling (Chapter Fourteen) making life sentences for juveniles unconstitutional is cause for hope. A lot of us plan to lobby the Maryland legislature to set a reasonable sentencing term for underage perpetrators. If this happens, I hope it will be retroactive to give Shanna a second chance at life.

"I'm lucky my family still loves me," Shanna told me. "At least they can visit me. [The victim's] parents have to go to her grave. They'll never forgive me."

People on both sides of the walls talk about forgiveness. Is it possible to forgive someone who hurt or, worse, killed your loved one? One saying I often hear is, "Not forgiving is like taking poison and expecting the other person to die." Rage, bitterness, and the lust for revenge have destroyed many lives.

DAPHNE

Daphne is one of the most educated people in our group. She attended a California college on full scholarship and was graduated with degrees in bookkeeping and economics and international relations. In 1991, she studied international financial and political risk analysis at Georgetown University and earned a Masters of Arts degree in Arab studies. She was accepted by the University of Baltimore Law School, but dropped out due to financial problems. She is sixty–four years old and has been in prison for sixteen years.

She does not like to talk about the events that led to her incarceration; all I know is that the victim is dead.

"When I was younger, I was an extremely shy person with little self–confidence. I was too trusting of others. After incarceration I realized I had to work on myself.

"I took more college classes and took advantage of self–help programs available in the prison such as Emotional Awareness and Cognitive Development. I participated in the Alternatives to Violence Project (AVP) and became a facilitator in the program. I have been a catalyst for new programs at the prison, including a Toastmasters group and guitar classes. The formation of I–WISH was my idea; I was the one who wrote to Mary Pat.

"I belong to a book club and a writers club and I'm active in W.H.O. (Women Helping Others). As part of W.H.O. I've assisted in activities such as Biggest Loser, Children's Book Day, and health fairs. I taught myself Spanish and can now carry on a conversation in that language.

"I like to read, remain active, and learn and accomplish new things. I write a lot of letters. Nothing gets by me. Sometimes this makes me unpopular among the officers or the other inmates."

This once "extremely shy" person has become one of the most outspoken people I have ever met. That, combined with her keen intelligence, makes her a valuable member of our group. She is always up to date on new laws that might affect lifers and is a wealth of information for her fellow prisoners. She is full of energy and will speak out against any actions she considers unjust or unfair.

Daphne was the first one to recognize the value FACES had to the participants as well as to their intended audience. She passed the lesson on to the kids:

> A funny thing happened while we were in rehearsal for this production. In the beginning, we wanted people to know us, to know that we are more than the things we did. But then, we began thinking more and more about *you*. And suddenly, you became what the play was all about. You became far more important than we were. We told ourselves: If we reach one kid, all our work will be worth it.
> And you know what happened? While we were working so hard to do something for you, we began to feel pretty good about ourselves. We were sitting a little straighter, walking a little bit taller, feeling a whole lot better about who we are. So, try it. Do something for somebody else. You might be surprised at how good it feels.

Daphne worries about her parents. "My parents still live

in California: my father is ninety–five and my mother is eighty–five. They still believe in my innocence and, in spite of numerous health problems, they come to Maryland twice a year to visit me. I hope to go home someday to be with them. They need me and are waiting for me."

With the help of therapy and the self–awareness programs, Daphne has matured and gained self–confidence. "I am no longer so gullible. I have learned to set healthy boundaries with relationships, and now I know I can make wise choices, on my own, no matter what the pressure from others."

What a shame she had to come to prison to find her voice.

JUDY

During the months I interviewed the women Judy always managed to avoid me, so I was surprised one evening when she handed me five typewritten sheets of paper. When I read her story that night, my first thought was, *This kid never had a chance.*

"The earliest memory I have of the abuse I suffered during my childhood was when I was four years old. My eleven–year–old brother was digging in burning trash and pulled out a stick with melted plastic dripping from it. He tossed it to me: 'Catch.' I caught it and the hot plastic ran over my thumb and the palm of my hand. I still have a scar on my thumb.

"My father and my nineteen–year–old brother started molesting me when I was eight. But my mother hurt me the most. She told me I was either stupid or retarded. I was fourteen–years–old when [a friend] submitted my name to the Miss Teenage Beauty Pageant. My mother said, 'You really don't think you have anything to offer or contribute, do you? You're not even that pretty. Someone must have played a joke on you.'

"My other brother was paralyzed from the chest down from an automobile accident. From age nine I took care of him. I changed his catheter and his diaper.

"There was not a day that my parents didn't argue and fight—usually about my dad cheating on my mom. They hit each other with their fists. Baseball bats, too. When I was sixteen, my mother slipped and fell on an icy driveway. I seen my dad look back and seen him back up and run over my mom's leg after knocking her down. He was going to do it again until I hit the side of his truck with my fist and told him I seen what he did and that I was telling.

"I got pregnant during my last year of high school. I didn't expect my mother to help me, but she offered to take me to a doctor. But the clinic she took me to was an abortion center. I wouldn't have the abortion and I married the father. My mother said, 'You might as well. No other man will ask you because you're damaged goods.' My first child, a boy, was born six months later.

"My husband went into military service and we were assigned to Iceland. I got pregnant again—this time with twins. That's when he began beating me. He told me he would buy anything the kids needed, but everything else would be my problem. He told me he only married me because it would cut his tour of duty in Iceland from three years to two. From Iceland, we were transferred to Scotland, where my husband would leave me and the kids alone for days. When he did come home, he beat me even more.

"When we got out of the service, we came back to Maryland. I thought at last I'd have contact with my family, but my husband threatened to kill me if I told anyone what was going on at home. He had trouble finding work. I went to work in a nursing home. Eighteen months later I was incarcerated for his murder.

"During my trial, a psychologist spoke in detail about my family history of abuse as a child and also by my husband. [The judge] said he [would hear the testimony] but it [would] not be admissible or be considered for my sentencing. He said there is no excuse for someone to take the life of someone else.

"I wholly agree. There is no excuse. Just like there is no excuse for anyone whether it be man or woman to abuse another person, physically, mentally, emotionally, or sexually."

Throughout her incarceration, Judy has taken advantage of all the self–help programs available. She has kept a job from the beginning of her term and she is infraction–free. She is a handler in the dog service–training program and intends to continue in the program upon her release.

As for her hopes for the future, Judy says, "I have completed some of the reentry programs which were a big help in learning how to use cognitive skills that were needed in my learning how to cope with abusive situations. I believe I am more than ready to return to society and I hope I will be given a second chance as I know I would be an asset to society once again."

TABBY

At age fourteen Tabby was a high school drop out estranged from her family, perfect material for the scumbag pimp who took her to local bars and taught her how to lure men outside with the promise of sex. The pimp, with the help of others of his ilk, would rob the victim and send him on his way. The robberies were seldom reported; no "decent" man wanted to admit to having sex with a fourteen–year–old child.

One robbery went too far and the victim died. All involved were sentenced to life in prison, including fourteen–year–old Tabby

In prison for thirty years, Tabby is no longer a child. She went to school, got her GED, and has dedicated her life to helping young inmates, trying to persuade them to avoid her fate. She developed a sense of self–worth denied to her as a child. She was one of the two people released after the passage of the 180–day bill (Chapter Fourteen). She is working and doing well.

Tabby was one of the performers in our production of FACES. She was a delight to watch—full of energy and always on cue. I used many of the lines from FACES in the first Kennedy Center production and she came to see the play. We met after the show and she wanted to congratulate the actors. I wasn't sure how to introduce her—I didn't feel it was my place to speak about her history.

Tabby solved my dilemma. She ran up to Tommy Malek—the actor who delivered the dialogue she had had in FACES—and threw her arms around him. "You did my lines! You were so good!" In an instant actor–to–actor bond, Tommy hugged her back.

MARGIE

Margie arrived early at a meeting some years back. We got to talking and she told me about her crime.

"I was sixteen years old and in love with a handsome boy. My cousin was in love with the same boy. We got into a fight. My cousin pulled a knife. I had a knife, too. A box–cutter. I cut my cousin, the fight ended, and I went home.

"Later that night, the police came to my house and took me to the police station. I wanted to call my mom. They told me it was just routine. They said, 'We just want to know about the fight. No need to call anyone.' I told them all about my cousin and the handsome boy. Then they told me my cousin was dead."

Margie was sentenced to life in prison.

CHAPTER TEN:
Prison Life

Everyday Details

It is my observation that the prison is a world within the world—again, similar to high school. As a teacher, I see the kids immersed in their adolescent lives, often completely oblivious to the world around them. They react to issues beyond themselves when they are on the "outside," or when "outsiders" invade their turf but, for the most part, their lives revolve around their families, their school activities, and their friends.

That's pretty much how I see the inmates live their lives, and I think it is the reason for their survival. As much as they miss the outside world they are no longer part of it, so they settle into an environment of their own. In some cases their real families have cut them from their lives and it is the women's way of coping with the loneliness. Sometimes I wonder why there aren't more suicide attempts, and then I realize the ability of human beings to adjust, and the desire to survive, is as alive in a prison as anywhere else. As in the rest of the world, hope is the last thing to die.

Jayna considered suicide several times. In FACES she described her last attempt:

> I broke the razor and climbed into my bunk with
> the blade in my left hand, legs crossed. I began a

delaying cut. I cut a small incision on my right
wrist. It stung a little. I flinched, and then the flesh
opened up with white meat against brown skin.
Red blood began to run down my arm. I waited.
Why wasn't I dead? I tried it again. Another slice.
Blood twinkling down again. Nothing happened.
At that moment I knew that it wasn't meant for
me to die. Something inside of me wanted to live,
even if it meant living the rest of my life in prison.

It is ironic that many of the women get into trouble
because they are rebelling against authority and control, and
then end up in a place where they have no choice but to
succumb to authority and no control over their lives. All of
their phone calls are recorded and any officer who deems it
necessary will read their mail. They are told when to get up,
when to eat, when to go to work, when to leave work, when
to exercise, when to go to the bathroom, and when to go to
bed. They lives are dictated and stepping out of bounds can
have drastic repercussions: tickets, loss of privileges, time on
lock, and, most far–reaching of all, a black mark on their
prison record that could affect the time they spend
incarcerated.

The rules are strict; the slightest infraction can result in
punishment: speaking disrespectfully to an officer, using foul
language, fighting with other inmates—anything that may
cause trouble in a maximum–security prison. The officers' job
is to keep them in line: to protect themselves, to protect the
women from each other, and to protect the public. *Security* is
the operative word. Whether they've been locked up for a
misdemeanor or a felony, they are criminals and some of
them have done terrible things.

Their credibility is shot. In a dispute between an inmate
and an officer, it is almost always assumed the inmate is lying.
There is no trust for the prisoners; quite often even their
families don't believe a word they say.

When a woman first arrives at the prison, she is issued a
number—a number that will be hers for life—and assigned to

lock for assessment. She is stripped and searched and permitted to keep only what she is wearing. In the case of a transfer from another prison, this regulation can lead to an unconventional manner of dress. Anything she had acquired in a previous prison must be left behind. The women know that, so they arrive at the prison wearing four or five layers of clothing, including underwear.

She is issued basic supplies: towel and washcloth, one set of sheets, one wool blanket, and a pillow. She receives a limited amount of clothing—not necessarily in the correct sizes: two pairs of socks, three pairs of underwear (bras and men's shorts), two denim jeans, two gray short–sleeved DPSCS gray t–shirts, one pair of tennis shoes, one robe, and one denim coat. No hats or hoodies allowed. She also receives a "care package:" toothpaste, toothbrush, soap, and shampoo. Local churches gather and donate the supplies; the prison chaplain supervises the distribution. She is allotted three rolls of toilet paper every other week. Three rolls sounds like enough to last two weeks, except that she is not given tissues or paper towels. She has to use the toilet paper for everything from blowing her nose to cleaning up spills and removing her makeup. If she gets a cold, she's out of luck.

In the past, families and friends were permitted to send packages. Due to contraband (usually drugs or cell phones) smuggled into the prison, that is no longer the case.

She must buy personal hygiene necessities and snack foods from the commissary, the prison "store." She must make a list for her once–a–week purchases, paid for with money she earns in her prison job or with funds sent by her family. She learns it is expensive to be in jail and that commissary quantities are limited. If an item is out of stock, she has to wait another week for shampoo, toothpaste, or a bag of salt and vinegar potato chips. Flower, fruit, or spice–scented lotions or creams are not available; they contain alcohol and are forbidden.

Twice a year she may order products from special prison catalogues. If her family sends money, she may buy anything from clothing to earrings (females only) to radios, clocks, and small television sets. She places orders from a list of permitted clothing with regulated prices. She cannot spend more than $6.00 for a bra, $4.00 for socks, or $5.29 for panties. Any lingering memories of Victoria's Secret lingerie are relegated to dreams.

Her total clothing inventory cannot exceed eight T–shirts, four pairs of pants (a combination of DPSCS gray sweat pants and jeans), three short–sleeved DPSCS shirts, two long–sleeved DPSCS shirts, four pairs of shoes, and one pair of earrings. Watches and wedding rings are allowed. All belongings are logged in. If she is found with an item not on her list, it is assumed stolen and immediately confiscated. A ticket and some time on lock inevitably follow.

Clothing styles are regulated. Nothing must resemble a uniform: no logos or patches. Any dark blue or black clothing she has is confiscated. Those are officers' uniform colors and the possession of either color of clothing is considered escape paraphernalia. No red: red and blue are gang colors. The restrictions regarding red or blue are so stringent I was not allowed to bring in red balloons for the Christmas party. I made a lot of Rudolph the Green Nose Reindeer. Anytime she leaves her cell she must be dressed in her gray prison clothing.

If she is new to the system, the loss of all electronic devices might be one of the most devastating deprivations. For the older women, incarcerated for thirty or forty years, it's not quite so bad. They didn't grow up with video games, computers, iPads, and cell phones glued to their ears. They didn't experience the Internet and the ability to have the world at their fingertips.

She doesn't have access to E–mail or to the Internet. She can apply for permission to use the library computers for word processing. If she is approved, she is permitted to use the computers once a week, an hour at a time. If she's lucky, her work will be saved on the computer. At times, however, when she logs on, whatever she is working on might be gone. It might be a computer glitch, or it could be that someone discovered her password and "accidentally" erased her document.

Following the newcomer's evaluation, a period of time that varies for each individual, she is assigned to a housing unit and a cell. Each wing of a housing unit—four wings in all—has two levels, twenty–four cells on each level. She enters via a front door that opens into a lobby area. The officers' glass–enclosed control module—otherwise known as the "bubble"—dominates the center of the space. Ten steps enclosed in a cage with a locked door lead to the elevated room. There are always two officers in the bubble and they always face opposite directions so they can surveil the activity below. The module is soundproofed; she will have to jump up and down and wave her arms to get an officer's attention.

She is taken to her wing. The four wings jut off the center in a bowtie fashion. Sliders separate the two sides of the building. One opens into wings A and B; on the opposite side of the lobby, another opens into wings C and D. Each wing has its own rec (recreation) area; a wall divides the space between the wings.

The showers are at the end of each wing near the telephone bank: about ten telephones per wing. She is allowed to call her family and friends, but the calls must be collect—expensive for the recipient— and she is limited to thirty minutes. Of course, that's only if the telephones are available, if the line isn't too long, and if the telephones are working.

She is shown the rec area in her wing. The space has tables and chairs for socializing, doing each other's hair, or playing cards or board games. There is one television set. A favorite show is *Cops*; the women cheer when the bad guys get busted. The shared television sometimes leads to arguments but, with no satellite dish or cable, the choices are limited so the arguments don't last long. Perhaps, if she's lucky, her family will surprise her with a small television of her own.

When she is led to her cell, she finds a small room, six by eleven feet: sixty–six square feet. She meets her roommate. She will have multiple roommates over the year and there is no distinction made between lifers and short–termers. Her roommate could be very nice or she could be a drugged–out addict or a person suffering emotional or mental instability. She has no choice in roommates.

Her cell has a heavy wooden door with a small rectangular window at the upper right–hand corner, approximately two feet by eight inches, a bunk bed, and two lockers. A toilet and a sink take up one corner of the room. A small mirror hangs over the sink. A shelf big enough for about ten books sits to the side of the mirror. On the wall to the outside there is an overhead window. It lets in some light, but doesn't do much for ventilation. There is no air conditioning; on summer nights she will experience temperatures in the nineties.

She is assigned one of the levels in the bunk bed and, when she sits on the bed, discovers it is a slab of metal with a thin, spongy, foam mattress. She may hear some of the women talk about the back problems they have due to the uncomfortable sleeping accommodations.

She is warned about infractions and told of the scale of severity involved in the punishment system, a defined and elaborate list of offenses and consequences. She is told to behave herself so she can earn (and keep) her "good days."

Good days can take time off a mandatory sentence. Like so many governmental issuances, the system is quite complicated. When an offender enters a prison, she is automatically granted two months of GCC (Good Conduct Credit); her mandatory release date is thereby moved up by two months. She can earn two more months for every year she serves—IF she doesn't break any rules.

And that's the difficult part. There are so many rules it doesn't take much to break one. Some of the rules appear a bit bizarre, but they are all reactive to something someone did in the past. For example, if she decides to cut her hair, she will be ordered to put the clippings into a plastic bag and hand the bag over to officers for disposal. Hair trimmings have been shaped into ropes or made into wigs.

The matrix of rules numbers from #100 to #400, with the #100 rules carrying the most severe penalties. The penalties are prescribed: X number of days in segregation for X infraction.

#100 infractions include the more egregious offenses that interfere with the daily operation of the prison: possessing weapons such as a razor pried out of a pencil sharpener; creating a disturbance or a riot; trying to escape or possessing escape paraphernalia; having a dirty urine specimen; or committing a sex act such as excessive masturbation or physical involvement with another inmate. Fighting is an automatic #100 offense even it is in self–defense. No matter what a fellow prisoner does to her, she must not fight back. A #100 infraction always carries a term in lock and always means the complete loss of any good days she has accumulated.

#200 infractions are less serious but still carry the mandatory loss of all good days. An example of a #200 infraction would be refusing to take part in a drug rehabilitation program or not completing it.

#300 infractions are anything that interferes with an officer's duty, such as disobeying one of the many signs posted around the prison: "Do not enter," "Out of Bounds," "If you want a ticket, come on in," "Do not sit on table," "You must have an appointment to enter," or "Do not move TV table or TV." #300 offenses also include petty theft, getting tattooed, possession of alcohol, or refusal to submit to a drug test.

#400 infractions are the least serious, but still carry some sort of punishment, perhaps limiting visitors or confinement to her cell for a number of days. These include such things as possession of lesser level contraband, which is anything she's not supposed to have: an onion, a tomato, a tin bowl, or a cigarette (no smoking allowed).

She can also earn good days by holding a prison job. The number of days is determined by the difficulty of the job. Going to school, working in the kitchen, serving as an observation aide for suicidal prisoners, cleaning toilets, or maintaining the grounds earns ten days per month; working as an orderly earns five days a month.

Assuming she has not reached the age of menopause, she will need supplies for her monthly cycle. Unless she can afford to buy tampons from the commissary (regular size only), she has to use sanitary napkins. The prison supplies one package of pads a month—twelve to a package. According to the women, the pads more resemble panty liners than sanitary napkins. If she has a heavy flow, she will have to beg other inmates for more. I was told they call out from their cells: "Anybody got any Bob Barkers?"

The Bob Barker company is one of the private organizations that packages and sells commissary merchandise. A new distributor took over the process recently and the cost of goods increased 4% to 1479% from prices charged just a year ago. The cost per item is far beyond the prices in the outside world. For tampons, a package of 18 pieces will cost an inmate $5.59 = $0.38/tampon. In the outside world, an on–line purchase of 36 pieces costs $6.99/package = $0.19/tampon.

Other prices are just as exorbitant: Tide® detergent pods are $7.99 for 14 pods = $0.57 per pod. On–line, a container of 57 pods costs $22.69 = $0.40/pod. Plastic spoons are another example: In prison, spoons are $0.10 each. On–line, a box of standard white plastic spoons runs $6.00 for 100 spoons = $0.06 each. At a Staples office supply store, the regular price for a box of 10 reams of typing paper—5000 sheets—is $45.99 = $0.009/sheet. With a $35 rebate, a $53.99 box of 10 reams sells for $19.99 = $0.004/sheet. In prison, a package of 200 sheets of typing paper is $4.50 = $0.02/sheet.

When the new distributor took over, healthy items that had once been available disappeared from the shelves, replaced by an increase in the amount of unhealthy snack foods. Gone are cranberry juice, fruit cups, pineapples, raisins, mixed nuts, peanuts, and protein powder. Instead, the shelves are stocked with potato chips and cheesy puffs. The dining hall does not have fresh fruits and vegetables except for bananas and pears. If our new inmate is put on a special diet, she may get an apple or an orange. As a result of the unhealthy carbohydrate diet she will gain weight—pounds that often lead to physical problems down the road.

As the years go on she is categorized by her behavior: Excellent, Good, Fair, or Poor depending upon the number and severity of infractions she incurs. Her standing will be of great importance when she is considered for parole.

She soon adapts to the daily routine. Lights on at 4:30 A.M. Some inmates are already awake; they set their clocks to get a jump on the shower line. Sometime between 5 A.M. and 6:15 A.M. she showers, dresses, and goes to the dining hall for breakfast, where the menu is a regulated cycle of meals.

She is assigned a job: kitchen, laundry, cleaning detail, office work, sewing, and data entry among others, or she may elect to go to school to complete her GED or work on her AA degree. Through her job she earns $1.25 a day. If she elects to do data entry, she is paid an additional $0.03 per one thousand keystrokes—about two hundred words. If she is in school, she will earn $0.95 per day.

If, due to illness or incapacity, she is unable to hold a job or go to school, she is classified as "indigent," and remains locked in her cell for the entire day. No job means no money unless her family helps her. No money means she cannot buy basic necessities from the commissary. She may receive one of the chaplain's care packages every ninety days. If she chooses to trade one of the hygiene items in return for unnecessary items such as candy or gum, she will lose that privilege.

When she returns from the dining hall after breakfast, she joins her fellow inmates in the rec area of her wing. She must stay in the area around her wing. Stepping into another area will result in a ticket. Between 6:25 and 6:45 A.M. the women are called according to their destinations. An officer uses her walkie–talkie to tell the receiving officer to, "stand by." Sometimes the "stand by" can stretch out to 20–30 minutes, but she has to stay in place until the housing officer gets the response, "Ready to receive." She is then allowed to leave the housing unit and she must leave at first call or risk a ticket. This is called "controlled movement" and it lives up to its name.

Between 7 and 7:30AM she is held at her destination for count—usually cleared by 8 or 9 A.M. At that time she may go to her individual area of employment or school. There she is counted again.

Lunch is served in the dining hall between 10:30 and 11 A.M., after which she resumes her work or school until 1:30 or 2:30 P.M. She returns to the housing unit and stays in the "rec" area or, in pleasant weather, remains outdoors to enjoy the fresh air or engage in a game of volleyball. At 3:30 P.M she must be in her housing unit, locked in her cell for a formal "stand–up ID count." This means she must stand by her door and be prepared to show her identification badge to the officers conducting the count.

At times there are activities scheduled after work, such as our play rehearsals, or she may have a medical or therapy appointment. She must arrange a pass for these events and her name must be included on a "movement sheet." She must be in place when count starts; no movement is allowed during the procedure.

Dinner follows the afternoon activities. If there are hamburgers or fried chicken on the dinner menu she will see smiles; those are the favorites. Most of the time, however, dinner is boiled meat and mushy vegetables.

Evening activities work the same way afternoon activities do. For example, on I–WISH nights an officer places a call to the housing units after Mary Pat, Susan, or I arrive. The women are allowed out of the units and must sign into the meeting when they get there. There are many evening activities: classes provided by Goucher College, Pilates, yoga, mother–and–baby classes, book clubs, Bible study, creative writing classes—most taught by volunteers or other inmates— and, most important, visits.

Visiting hours are from 5 to 8 P.M. on weekdays, and 8 A.M. to 2 P.M. and 5 to 8 P.M. on weekends. Our inmate's visiting day will depend upon the last digit of her prison number: even number: even–numbered days; odd number: odd–numbered days. No visits on the thirty–first of a month in order to keep the number of visiting days equal. Visiting days are Thursday through Monday; no visits on Tuesday and Wednesday. She is allowed eight visits per month. Her visitor list is limited to fifteen people and the chaplain must approve the list. Those under age eighteen are not included in the limited number.

If she has children, she is allowed to see them on regular visiting days. Any hugs or other physical contact must be done across a table. She is not permitted to cuddle the children—including babies—in her lap. The children often cry because they are not allowed to go to their mothers. They must remain on the other side of the barrier.

All activities must end promptly at 9 P.M. so she can be back in her cell for the 9:30 P.M. formal count. At 10:30 P.M. there is an informal count. At 11 P.M. everyone is locked in her cell. At 11:30PM there is another count. Usually this is not a "stand–up" count; the officers will watch for movement if she is asleep. Lights out at midnight on weekdays, at 1 A.M. on weekends.

If she goes infraction–free for a year, she may earn her way onto the "honor pod." This is a special housing unit that is less guarded and has minimal supervision. The cell doors open at 8 A.M. and stay open until 9 P.M. except for the 3:30 P.M. formal count. On weekends and holidays she is allowed out of her cell from 12 noon until 2 A.M.

If she gets into trouble and sent to "lock," she will be subject to the rules for the "seg" units described in Chapter One. Upon release from lock, she will return to regular housing. It will take her more than a year of perfect behavior to earn her way back onto the honors unit.

Showering—keeping clean—is an important part of prison life. The newer housing units have more up–to–date facilities but, according to the women, the older units are a nightmare—moldy and infested with bugs. The temperature of the water is pre–set. Whatever comes out of the showerhead is what she will get. Sometimes the water is freezing cold—unpleasant in the winter.

The shower stalls are in the hallway, covered with curtains that billow away from the spraying water. She must hang her robe outside the stall before she enters. The curtain only covers her from neck to mid–calf. The showers are on the first level. Officers on the second level can easily look down into the area. When a male officer is on duty, this can be humiliating.

Laundry day is once a week on a rotating schedule. She must buy her detergent at the commissary and she will be limited to two loads. With the curbed clothing allowance, this is usually enough. Inmates assigned to the laundry room operate the machines.

Violence among the female prisoners in no way matches that among the men. There are fights and rare violent actions but, for the most part, it's a fairly calm place—at least when I am there. The officers have to be careful, but they tell me they don't feel the same tension when they are with the women as they do with the men, although when I came up behind an officer I had befriended and tapped her on the shoulder, she jumped. I was admonished by a senior officer and told to never do that again.

A large sense of resentment on the women's part stems from the treatment they receive when there is a disturbance in the men's side. The women suffer the same consequences and receive whatever punishment the men get. Usually this involves a lockdown until peace is restored, and the lockdown can last for days. The worst part of this: no visitors. This is rough on the visitors as well. Many families and friends travel miles to visit their loved one. There is no way to notify people of a lockdown, so they have to leave without seeing the person they came to see.

It is heart–wrenching to see the visitors in the gatehouse—especially the children. Often there are tiny babies who were born in the prison and turned over to fathers, aunts, uncles, grandparents, or foster homes. The toddlers are usually frightened by the uniformed officers even though the officers do their best to put the children at ease. The metal detector is another intimidating thing for the little ones and the pat down almost always produces tears. It is unbelievably sad and I have to wonder what desperation the women were facing when they committed their crimes and risked being taken away from these beautiful children.

In our play's two–year run, we had a series of public performances every few months. We couldn't perform in the summer because, other than the offices, the prison is not air–conditioned. Maryland summers are hot and humid. We experience hundred–plus–degree–days with humidity so high it feels like swimming through lukewarm Jell–O.

In hot weather the gym feels like a sauna. Two six–foot fans sit at either end of the gym, but all they do is swirl the heat around the room. And they are noisy. We had performances in early June and had to turn the fans off for the duration of the play so the actors could be heard. By the time we got through, sweat was staining our shirts and audience members were wiping their brows.

A nice, cool iced drink is, for the most part, out of the question. There are ice machines, but they often break down in the excessive heat. In FACES, Talia talks about ice for prison inmates:

> It was a hot, humid, Code 2 day. Two inmates got into a fight and the officers took the ice points away from everyone in the vicinity, so the rest of us didn't get any ice in our drinks. We have to earn points to get frozen water.

I think of that every time I get a scoop of ice from my refrigerator.

The lifers' attitude toward time took me by surprise. To them, a year is a flicker in the long passage of their lives. Cassie, an inmate from out–of–state—a short–termer—offered to coach the actors during the off hours. She has a Masters Degree in theater. I have no idea what she had done to get herself locked up; all I knew was the women needed all the help they could get. And I can only imagine how grateful Cassie was to have the opportunity to work in her own field. She was not permitted to join I–WISH. The group is strictly for lifers—the only prison organization devoted exclusively to problems they face.

At a rehearsal several weeks later, I asked, "How are things going with Cassie?"

"She's gone. She's been transferred to prerelease," Clarinda told me.

"That's wonderful," I said. "So she'll be going home soon?"

"She sure is," Clarinda said. "Won't be long. Eighteen months, two years — no time at all."

Eighteen months, two years—no time at all?

The same thing happened when another short–termer was denied parole. The women talked about how badly they felt for her.

"But we told her it wouldn't be long before she could appeal again. Three or four years, tops," one of them said.

For a lifer, the years meld together.

CHAPTER ELEVEN:
Life After Prison

The Nightmare is Over—Not

If our inmate is a short–termer, she will eventually be released. It is a joyful time. She's going home. Lots of goodbyes, good luck wishes, tearful embraces, and gentle reminders to stay out of trouble and not come back.

She walks through the sliding gates a free woman. No more Correctional Officers telling her when to eat and when to go to the bathroom. No more canned peas. She can open doors all by herself, ride in a car, go to a restaurant, eat a biscuit, walk on the beach, wear a red shirt, and have all the ice she wants.

In many cases she spends some time in a halfway house, a living situation designed to help her reentry into the outside world. She is still restricted and subject to rules, regulations, and drug testing, but she can walk in the sunshine and enjoy her freedom. The nightmare is over.

Except it isn't.

Reality sets in. She is an ex–con. In the eyes of the world she will always be a criminal.[8] The path she must take to rebuild her life is a long and arduous journey.

---

[8]For an excellent discussion of the realities of post prison life, I highly recommend *The New Jim Crow: Mass Incarceration in the Age of Colorblindness* by Michelle Alexander. The New Press. New York, NY.

She applies for a job and faces her first wall: the little box on the application form: *Have you ever been convicted of a crime?* When she is released from the halfway house she finds another wall when she tries to rent an apartment. Few landlords want to rent to an ex–offender and the rules for subsidized housing bar anyone who has served time in prison. Perhaps she overcomes these obstacles, finds a good job, a place to live, and saves up enough money for a down payment on a house. What bank is going to take the risk of granting a mortgage to someone with a criminal background?

She can lie, but it won't do much good. One flick of the fingers across a computer keyboard reveals her record to anyone who cares to look for it. There are movements across the country to "Ban the Box,"[9] making it illegal for a prospective employer to ask about criminal activities on a job application. But even if she gets past the initial interview and is offered a job, the inevitable background search will follow and the offer may be withdrawn. Or she may get the job, work for a few months, and then get fired when the employer discovers her record.

Perhaps she decides to get involved in politics and work to change some of the broken policies of our judiciary system. She can make speeches, testify on Bills in her state's capitol, and campaign for her favorite candidate. However, in many states she is not allowed to vote. According to Attorney General Eric Holder, "Across this country today, an estimated 5.8 million Americans … are prohibited from voting because of current or previous felony convictions…. That's more than the individual populations of 31 U.S. states."[10] Maryland repealed the restriction in 2007.[11]

2012.

[9]"Ban the Box bill advances over opposition from businesses." By Yvonne Wenger. *The Baltimore Sun.* April 7, 2014.

[10]Holder: Change laws to let ex–convicts vote." By Kevin Johnson. *USA Today.* February 11, 2014.

[11]"Felons gain right to vote." by Andrew A. Green. *The Baltimore Sun.* April 25, 2007.

There are many services across the country designed to help returning citizens deal with reentry. One of the best is the Prison Outreach Ministry Welcome Home Reentry Program, an agency dedicated to "Opening doors to help and hope." It is part of the nonprofit Pre–Release Services Center in Rockville, Maryland, one of many programs that has given Montgomery County national recognition for its progressive ideas in social issues. Under the auspices of the Catholic Charities Archdiocese of Washington in cooperation with the Maryland Correctional Office, Welcome Home is so successful The National Association of Counties named it a 2008 Achievement Award Winner, "In recognition of an effective and innovative program [that] contributes to and enhances the county government in the United States."

FRED CHANDLER

Fred Chandler is the Reentry Coordinator for the Welcome Home program. His path to what he calls "his ministry" took a convoluted route.

In 1968, Mr. Chandler enrolled in the University of Pennsylvania, one of only sixty–eight African–Americans in a student body of twenty thousand, and a different world from the one he had known growing up on the streets of Philadelphia. An avowed militant, he was active in the Black Power movement, including the Black Panthers. He divided his time between school studies and political demonstrations.

Short on funds, he dropped out of college and embarked on a succession of jobs that took him to the West Coast and back.

In 2005 he went to work for Laborfinders managing a placement service for day laborers. That job led to developing programs for job training, job readiness, job search, and job retention at the Montgomery County Correctional Facility in Boyds, Maryland.

In 2008 he started work with MontgomeryWorks as coordinator of the REBOUND Reentry Program where he served as liaison for Montgomery College, MontgomeryWorks, and the Montgomery County Pre–Release Services Center. He found his niche.

At the entrance to the Pre–Release Center, a sculpture greets me: *Starting a New Life*: a man, lunch box in hand, kissing his wife goodbye. Inside the front door, a cafeteria and offices flank the right and left sides of the lobby.

There are 150 carefully screened residents at the Center, nonviolent and violent offenders placed there by judicial decree to live out their prison sentences, usually three to nine months before their scheduled release. According to Mr. Chandler, women are convicted of ten percent of the crimes in Montgomery County; the Center's population reflects that percentage.

A new resident is given thirty days to find employment, a period that can be extended if he has shown diligence in seeking a job. Upon hire, he is required to remit twenty percent of his salary to the Center; another percentage goes to a savings account available to him upon his release.

He lives under close scrutiny. He is only allowed out to work or to seek work and must submit to daily drug tests. He may be released to home confinement, but he is required to report back to the Center one to three times a week, more often if he has a history of drug use. He is assigned a housekeeping chore, anything from cleaning to cooking to maintaining the grounds.

The four units that make up the living quarters are each equipped with a lounge and a television. Residents have individual rooms and, in a radical change from prison, the key to those rooms. Each room has a toilet and a sink and is inspected daily. There are no locked doors between the units or to the outside, but trespassing onto another unit or leaving the Center without permission can result in a write–up. Outside, the grounds are beautifully kept, with attractive greenery and colorful flowers, and a vegetable garden.

Upon entry, a newcomer is assigned a Work Release Coordinator who tracks his job performance and stays in touch with his employers, and a Case Manager who oversees his reentry plans and monitors his behavior on and off the job. Though they do not wear uniforms, these staffers are Correctional Officers. They have the power to write up residents for infractions and, in the case of a severe violation, return them to prison to complete their sentences.

The walls in the corridors are filled with brightly colored and informative signs: job openings, educational opportunities, trips to museums or community service projects, help with resumes, classes for fathers, and GED programs. There are two computer rooms, with twenty computers the residents may use for researching employment or training. There is a medical facility with a nurse on duty and a doctor on call. Across the courtyard, there is a second building with classrooms and meeting rooms.

As the Reentry Coordinator, Mr. Chandler helps residents prepare resumes. Often, skills learned in prison can be applied to jobs in the outside world, as is the case with "Mike" (below).

He also coordinates the mentor program. Volunteers commit to a year of companionship with an ex–offender who might benefit from the mentor's experience. Clients and mentors are carefully matched and the volunteers work closely with the ex–offenders, offering friendship and encouragement. According to Mr. Chandler, if the relationship is maintained—often going beyond the one–year commitment—the risk of recidivism is significantly reduced. In the United States, the general recidivism rate averages sixty–eight percent; recidivism for the Welcome Home Reentry Program's mentees is twenty percent.

The most important—and perhaps most difficult—thing an ex–offender must learn is how to be forthright about his criminal background. He must be transparent about his past—tell prospective employers about his crime(s) before the employers discover the truth themselves and assume the worst. With Mr. Chandler's help, he prepares his "Letters of Explanation," which must include three important points:

- Admitting his crime
- Taking responsibility for the crime and not placing the blame on anyone else
- Explaining why it won't happen again

Some clients "stonewall" Mr. Chandler and refuse to discuss their pasts: "I don't want to talk about it," they say. Mr. Chandler worries for them: "If they can't talk to me, how can they talk to employers?"

A big problem Mr. Chandler sees in our penal system is the too–generous dispensing of sedatives and tranquilizers. "Mental health issues are not addressed in a proper and professional way. Many offenders have a lot of mental baggage, and county, state, and local prison staffs are not equipped to handle [their illnesses]. They dispense drugs to keep the inmates quiet and under control. The system has taught [the prisoners] to self–medicate. Upon release, they get drugs on the street. The practice enables a drug–addictive lifestyle."

The Welcome Home program lends itself to Mr. Chandler's theory: "Preparation for reentry should begin on the first day of incarceration. When offenders are prepared, they develop a life different from the streets and are less likely to repeat their crimes. It works."

SUCCESS STORIES

Tina spent time in prison for dealing drugs to support her own habit. When Mr. Chandler first met her, her appearance showed the results of that disease: malnourished body and disheveled hair covered with a cheap wig that often turned sideways. She cleaned herself up and became an expert at preparing resumes. After landing a series of good jobs, she went back to school. She is six years drug–free and a counselor in Frederick, Maryland.

Lynn served twelve years in a federal prison for drug peddling. She came out with the desire to change and the energy to do it. She learned how to present herself, how to look for a job, and how to be forthright about her past. A born leader, she trained in mediation counseling. She is excelling in two jobs: one in a supermarket, the other in a restaurant.

Mike had been incarcerated for twenty years for a violent crime. He worked in the prison kitchen, rising from cook to kitchen manager, supervising the preparation of nine hundred meals a day. After two interviews with the owner of a prominent D.C. restaurant, he was hired. "I don't care about his record," the owner said. "I needed a manager. If he can serve nine hundred meals a day, I can use him. Maybe he can serve nine hundred meals a day in my restaurant!"

CHAPTER TWELVE:
Human Trafficking

A Worldwide Menace

You're in a 1950s movie theater. The screen lights up with a familiar scene: bearded men with cruel beady eyes, dressed in voluminous robes and flowing headpieces, surrounded by beautiful women lounging by a pool wearing skimpy belly dancer outfits. Perfect picture of Hollywood's twentieth-century version of human trafficking.

Now shine the lights on twenty–first–century reality: thousands of girls and boys in pajama bottoms and t-shirts, some as young as eleven years old, for sale to the highest bidder. Sex–based human trafficking is rampant all over the world, including the United States.

The only things—and I use this word advisedly—scummier than the drug dealers who sell their poison to children are the scumbag thugs who enslave young boys and girls in prostitution. They are the personification of evil. I have to wonder what kind of childhoods they had and what kind of abuse they suffered to turn them into the vile predators they are.

I talked with Lamont Carey, an ex–offender who served time for drug dealing, came out of prison, rebuilt his life, and went on to become a successful inspirational speaker. He talked to me about one of the side affects of domestic abuse.

As a child, Mr. Carey witnessed the abuse his father inflicted upon his mother: beatings, lies, cheating, and betrayal. He couldn't understand why his mother stayed in the home. He lost all respect for her, which led to a lack of respect for all women. Perhaps this legacy applies to the subhuman pimps as well.

Statistics for human trafficking are limited. There are few data points and no unified studies. The laws vary from county to county, state to state, and country to country. If a prostituted girl is arrested in one county or state, her pimp moves her to another. The available statistics, while alarming, are incomplete because of countless unreported incidences. There are numerous anecdotal reports, but no empirical evidence to fully determine the scope of this widespread scourge.

However, in Googling *human trafficking*, I found the following information—all of it with the caveat of unreported cases and incomplete statistics.

THE POLARIS PROJECT
FOR A WORLD WITHOUT SLAVERY

The Polaris Project is a leading organization in the global fight against human trafficking and modern–day slavery. Named after the North Star "Polaris" that guided people escaping slavery along the Underground Railroad, Polaris Project is transforming the way that individuals and communities respond to human trafficking, in the U.S. and globally. By successfully pushing for stronger federal and state laws, operating the National Human Trafficking Resource Center hotline (NHTRC 1–888–373–7888), conducting trainings, and providing vital services to victims of trafficking, Polaris Project creates long–term solutions that move our society closer to a world without slavery.[12]

THE NATIONAL HUMAN TRAFFICKING RESOURCE CENTER (NHTRC)

The NHTRC hotline received reports of 9,298 unique cases of human trafficking across the United States in its first five years of operation, Polaris Project announced in a new report today. The report, *Human Trafficking Trends in the United States*, includes one of the most extensive sources of human trafficking data in the country. From December 7, 2007 to December 31, 2012, cases of human trafficking were reported in all 50 states and D.C. More than 42% of sex trafficking cases referenced pimp–controlled prostitution, and more than 27% of labor trafficking cases referenced domestic work. The statistics from the report are based solely on the more than 72,000 interactions made to the NHTRC through phone calls, emails, and online tip reports, indicating that the full scope of the problem in the United States is significantly larger.

People are reaching out to the national human trafficking hotline every single day and telling us that modern slavery is happening in their communities," said Bradley Myles, CEO of Polaris Project. "Girls are forced by pimps to sell sex at truck stops. Domestic workers are abused by their employers. Men are isolated on farms with limited access to food and water. This report demonstrates that traffickers are not operating in just one city or region. We have identified potential cases of human trafficking in every state

---

[12]polarisproject.org.

in the nation."[13]

From its inception on December 7, 2007 through December 31, 2012, the hotline operated by the Polaris Project answered 65,557 calls, 1,735 online tip forms, and 5,251 emails. The numbers below are based on information learned from those interactions.

- The NHTRC experienced a 259% increase in calls between 2008 and 2012.
- In five years they received reports of 9,298 unique cases of human trafficking.
- 41% of sex trafficking cases referenced U.S. citizens as victims.
- Women were referenced as victims in 85% of sex trafficking cases.
- 33% of victims of sex trafficking were minors.
- There were 2,668 child trafficking cases reported.[14]

The majority of sex–based human trafficking recruiters are pimps. Older—more senior—prostitutes called "bottom girls" assist them. The term refers to the fact that the pimp is always the one on top—the boss. The bottom girls train and supervise the new recruits and can be just as ruthless and cruel as the pimps themselves.

The pimps and their flunkies troll for vulnerable boys and girls everywhere: socially, through friends or at a party; in public places such as shopping malls, playgrounds, libraries, middle school, high school, and college campuses, train and bus stations and on the streets; online; in residential group homes; in homeless shelters; in bars and clubs; in detention facilities; in rehab centers; in foster homes—anywhere they can find lonely and susceptible children.

They are experts at spotting them. Maybe the kids are alone, or they are with friends but obviously not a part of the

---

[13]National Sexual Violence Resource Center HUMAN TRAFFICKING STATISTICS WASHINGTON, D.C. November 21, 2013. nsvrc.org.
[14]polarisproject.org.

group, or they are fighting with their parents, or they are hooking school, or they are runaways. So many young people, just there, perfect targets for the vultures.

They swoop down and promise anything their prey wants to hear: a loving relationship, a fantastic job that will make them famous. *You can be a supermodel! You can be a star!* If the kids look homeless and lost they offer food, shelter, and money. Anything to hook them. Anything to get the innocent young victims into their clutches.

Then comes the "If you love me...." gambit. *If you love me, you will strip. If you love me, you will turn a few tricks.* It doesn't take long. Before they know it, the girls are trolling at truck stops and performing sex acts with the "fine upstanding men and solid citizens" who pay the pimps—not the girls—for the services.

Next comes the violence: withholding food and shelter if the girls don't earn their quota for the day, and beatings and threats to kill them and their families if they try to leave. *I'll find you wherever you go. You cannot hide from me.* The pimps will say and do anything to keep the girls on the streets and raking in the money these contemptible men spend on their fancy cars and sparkling jewelry. They need the cars and the bling to attract more girls into "The Life."

Fortunately, there are good men, too. Fifty–seven percent of the tips provided to the hotline regarding minor victims came from truck drivers. One driver said, "As a trucker I've been approached by young girls at truck stops across the country. Every time I call NHTRC. And every time NHTRC is quick to respond."[15]

JEANNE ALLERT

One of the leading figures in the fight against this abomination is Jeanne Allert. She is the founder and executive director of The Samaritan Women (TSW), a residential center for survivors of human trafficking. TSW is located on a

---

[15]polarisproject.org.

twenty–three–acre farm in Baltimore—the largest farm in the city. I went there to interview Ms. Allert, planning to include her in Chapter Thirteen along with other people I have met on this incredible journey. What she told me about human trafficking was so shocking it inspired this chapter.

Upon arrival at The Samaritan Women I met first with Mr. Jon Fichman, the Director of Philanthropy and Finance, and Ms. Marie Hardy, bookkeeper for the organization. They greeted me warmly and turned me over to Ms. Melissa Yao, one of the anti–trafficking specialists employed at TSW. Ms. Yao took me on a tour of the farm and told me the fascinating history of the organization's beginnings.

In 2007 Ms. Allert and a partner decided to open a center for traumatized women to offer emotional, physical, and spiritual healing. They were looking for a venue in Baltimore when they got lost. They drove into a driveway to turn around and discovered an abandoned estate. And it was for sale.

They contacted the owner, a West Virginian who came from a family that owned a great deal of real estate. Ms. Allert and her partner inquired about the property and learned there was a $1.6 million bid on it, with plans to convert it into an assisted–living facility. They offered all they could afford: $500,000. So taken by their mission, the owner accepted the offer.

Then came another twist: Ms. Allert's business partner dropped out, leaving Ms. Allert with a choice: walk away from the project or take a huge leap of faith and go forward. "I prayed nonstop," Ms. Allert told me, "until the answer was clear." In October 2007, the story of The Samaritan Women began.

And so she had the property: twenty–three acres upon which sat two dilapidated houses, one built in the late nineteenth century; the other in the 1920s.

The nineteenth–century dwelling had once been a mansion. Then it became a mental hospital. Then it became a convenient place for the homeless. The neighborhood teenagers called it, "the haunted mansion on the hill." Part of the house had burned, the front porch was falling off, and there were piles of garbage left behind by hoarding squatters. They found remnants of the mental hospital as well: electroshock therapy equipment and restraints. The newer house, once a beautiful family home, was in complete disrepair as well. There was no way anyone could enter either place safely, let alone live there.

Enter thousands of community volunteers, mobilized by Ms. Allert's vision for a place of healing. They tore down, rebuilt, and cleaned out. They restored a beautiful antique mirror and a valuable stone fireplace and hauled away tons of garbage. The process took four years. The mansion became the residence for the survivors. The family home gave TSW offices and spaces for counseling and conferencing.

In 2011 the first residents moved in. TSW now has a fourteen–bed capacity. It receives referrals from all over the country and is often full. The residents may stay for up to two years at no charge. In addition to shelter, the program provides food, clothing, counseling, case management, recreation, and academic and vocational support. There are limitations as to whom they can accept: the women must be eighteen or older and they must be stabilized from any substance abuse.

This is not a prison; it is a home. The residents live together as a community. They may apply for on–site internships that provide minimum wage and valuable job skills. The Samaritan Women offers training, education, and, most important, healing. Some of the things they must learn are basic skills for survival in society—skills they never acquired such as how to balance a checkbook, clean a floor, or write a resume.

The program has three pillars:

1. The Residence Program offers services to help the women heal from their trauma, regain their self–esteem, grow spiritually, and learn skills that will enable them to reenter society.

2. The Maryland Rescue and Restore Coalition is The

Samaritan Women's statewide anti–human trafficking program. With help from citizens all across Maryland, the coalition seeks to raise public awareness, provide industrial training, increase victim identification and referrals, and help coordinate victim services.

3. The TSW farm is an important part of the healing process. It is fully functional and provides food for the residents who plant and care for the crops. Any surplus food is donated to agencies that provide fresh produce to impoverished inner–city families with limited funds or no access to supermarkets.

My next step was to meet with Ms. Allert. She is a lively woman with an office overflowing with projects. She was born in the small town of Waukesha, Wisconsin. Her father was an administrator for The International School system; her mother a stay–at–home mom. When she was eight years old the family moved overseas, moving from country to country as her father's position dictated. All in all, she lived in forty-six countries, including Thailand and Iran.

She admits to having a charmed life. She had the means and the freedom for travel, education, and fulfilling employment. This foundation of privilege led her to establish The Samaritan Women.

"There was a point where I hit a wall of affluence," she told me. "I realized life only has value if you give it away." Her life took a radical turn when, at age forty, she was moved by the Bible verse, *To whom much is given, much more is expected.*[16] "I left the pursuit of external happiness to devote myself to improving the lives of others."

According to Ms. Allert, systemic issues make solving the problem of domestic sex–based human trafficking difficult. One is the lack of public awareness. "Most people just don't know this is an American problem. And Americans are contributing to the exponential growth of this illegal industry because of our appetite for products and sex. The Maryland

---

[16]*Luke 12:48.*

Rescue and Restore Coalition is working to raise the level of awareness and give citizens constructive ways to deal with the problem."

She also pointed out that most states have no mandate to train law enforcement officials as to how to deal with the prevalence of human trafficking or how to spot the victims. "Even though federal law asserts that anyone under the age of eighteen is automatically considered a victim, in most jurisdictions a prostituted teenager is considered a criminal, not a victim. This misidentification is complicated by the fact that police are trained to look for drug activity, but not trained to ask the kind of screening questions that might suggest a case of human trafficking. Law enforcement officers are only going to see what they're looking for."

The women who come to The Samaritan Women need healing, hope, and regrowth in order to reclaim their lives. Over the years TSW has learned it's not just the trauma associated with being trafficked that must be addressed. Most of the women suffered years of abuse, neglect, and exploitation before being trafficked. Ninety–eight percent of the women TSW serves were molested as children. Seventy percent come from fatherless homes, often rife with violence and substance abuse. About half of the women struggle with substance abuse and self–inflicted injuries.

Intensive counseling is essential. At the beginning Ms. Allert had no training in the field. She embarked on a course of on–the–job–training. She sought out psychologists, authors, and medical practitioners all over the U.S. and partnered with a veteran survivor, who became her best "professor." Most of all, she relies on her faith and what she's learned from walking with these women, every day, all day, for the past three years. Now the women call her, "the best counselor they ever had."

The Samaritan Women's therapeutic approach includes three stages:

Stage One focuses on safety and stability. When a woman first comes to TSW, she's often "very rough." She's fearful and guarded. She relies on survival skills she learned on the streets. She's volatile and emotional.

"Our efforts need to concentrate on providing her with a sense of safety in the environment—with the people, and with the program. We have to help her feel safe within herself because in the first ninety days the 'flight response' is acute," Ms. Allert said. "Most people make the mistake of thinking that 'loving up on them' is what they need at this stage, but the truth is what they need most is structure and routine.

"They need to detox from the chaos that has been their life. We focus a lot on household routines, sobriety, coping and communication skills, and individual and group counseling. It is almost a deprogramming process. Survivors have to 'unlearn' things they were taught: *I'm your daddy. I love you.* The pimps were never their 'daddies' and they never loved them. It is traumatic for the women to have to accept the fact that the people they had trusted for most of their lives had never loved them.

"We also use peer support. Someone who has been through what they've been through can offer not only empathy, but also reality. We call it 'talking them out of their crap.' Often only another woman who has had the same experience can relate and speak the truth into her life."

By Stage Two the survivors have established a sense of stability and they embark on a journey of discovery. According to the TSW staff, this stage is the most fun. The women are willing to try all those things they never experienced earlier in life. TSW offers an array of opportunities; community volunteers provide even more. TSW becomes a safe space for the residents to explore art, music, fitness, gardening, reading, cultural events, and all types of play therapy.

"Part of the reason we don't jump into academics or vocation right off the bat is because they haven't even discovered who they are. On average, they've spent four to eight years in The Life, being the person someone else demanded them to be. They need the time to become themselves. This is also the stage where they are the most open spiritually. They are ready to ask challenging questions about God. They open their minds to the idea that a New Life is actually possible."

By Stage Three the survivors are becoming more comfortable. They are settling into their personal choices and working on developing commitment and perseverance. At this stage TSW offers opportunities to add responsibility through the internship program, online education tutoring, or other job training. "If they choose to do so, they can advocate on the issue of human trafficking," Ms. Allert said. "We've engaged survivors in researching human trafficking, speaking to the public, and testifying on antitrafficking legislation. All of this is empowering. They learn they are no longer victims and can use their experiences to help others."

Ms. Allert summed up TSW's mission:

> The Samaritan Women is about rebuilding a woman's resilience. Whether it was through traumatic childhood experiences, environment, or personal choices, she was victimized because she was made vulnerable. We must replace vulnerability with resilience, including a relationship with God, a stronger sense of self, personal accomplishments, friendships, and coping skills. Without that foundation she's only going to leave here and be re–victimized. We know, if she uses this time to secure internal strength and external support, she will go out and offer those gifts to others. What we're creating here are women of resilience who will have an impact on the world.

According to Ms. Allert, "Betsy's" story is typical of "How A Girl Gets Sucked into The Life."

Betsy came from an affluent suburban home. Chubby as a child, she was ridiculed and ignored by her peers. She turned to sex and "bad boys" as a substitute for the attention she craved. Her behavior became so outrageous her desperate parents sent her to live with a relative in an attempt to remove her from her toxic environment.

But being half way across the country didn't make Betsy immune to exploitation. Her vulnerabilities went with her. It wasn't long before she met a new "bad boy." This one knew The Game and played the "If you love me…" card. He talked her into stripping, which led to turning tricks, which led to living the life of a prostitute.

For six years her pimp prostituted her all over the West Coast. During that time it was as if she had a veil over her eyes that blinded her to the reality of her life. *Everything is going to be fine. After all, he loves me. We just need to make a little money—enough to have the life we both want.*

But, like all pimps, his only interest in her was the money she could earn for him. She was traded from predator to predator, ending up with a "gorilla pimp," the nastiest and most brutal of them all.

Over time the veil began to lift. She realized the promised good life was never to be and looked for a way out. By then, however, she had been arrested so many times she knew her record would keep her from having a "normal" life. And she knew that defying her pimp in any way would bring on more beatings.

After multiple trips to the emergency room and a near-death experience, she met a detective who had been trained in human trafficking and was familiar with The Game. He made her look at the truth. "If you go on like this," he told her, "the next time I see you, you will be dead." She accepted his help. He took her to a secure safe house and the shelter's staff contacted The Samaritan Women.

Now twenty-six years old, Betsy has been at TSW for almost a year. She has re-established ties with her family and is attending college with plans to become a lawyer.

"There is some awesome healing going on there," Ms. Allert told me.

A pro bono attorney is working with Betsy to get her charges expunged. Perhaps most significant of all, she has garnered the courage to testify against her former pimp. With the theory of a prostitute as a victim and therefore entitled to civil remedy, she is seeking restitution from the soul–sucking predator who stole years from her life. She is learning to stand tall and appreciate herself. She is reclaiming her life.

"Betsy is a perfect example of someone who is going to go back out into the world bearing her scars, but using them to make a profound impact on others," Ms. Allert told me. "She and others like her are why we do what we do."

CHAPTER THIRTEEN:
Tragedy and Courage

Other people I met

I've learned a lot in the years since that life–changing telephone call in May 2008. I'm still learning. Some of this knowledge solidifies my views as a knee–jerk, bleeding–heart, anti–gun, anti–death penalty, Bambi–loving, tree–hugging, liberal Democrat. Other things I see and learn challenge those views. The conflict and confusion lead to a lot of sleepless nights.

Like other people, I read newspaper headlines and watch television shows about unspeakable crimes. The devastation of the victims' families is heartbreaking and I can't help but feel their pain. The perpetrators' mug shots depict wild–eyed monsters—despicable people from whom society must be protected. I'm glad they were caught and prosecuted, and I am grateful to the justice system for removing them from my safe little world.

Then, a few months after their convictions, I meet one of these "monsters" and I'm blown away by their "normalness." This person sitting across the table from me committed a heinous crime, is deservedly in prison, and we are having a friendly discussion about my new sneakers. Myriad adjectives fill my mind: weird, bizarre, surreal, freaky, all of which feed my confusion. I drive home from the prison with tears in my eyes, feeling guilty about leaving my friends behind, wishing I could take them with me. Then it hits me again: They killed somebody.

The topic of "second chances" almost always comes up in meetings. The lifers have taken giant steps towards understanding themselves and what led to the circumstances of their crimes and incarceration. They've had psychological treatment, taken anger–management classes, earned their GED and AA degrees, and are completely different people from the angry young women they once were. Do they deserve a second chance at a life beyond prison? Their victims have no such opportunity. Why should they?

Along the way, it has been my privilege to meet incredible people on both sides of the issue. For various reasons they became involved in the judicial system and, with courage and perseverance, they strive for what they consider fair treatment for perpetrators, for victims and their loved ones, and for society. Each person I interviewed had his or her own reasons for involvement in the criminal justice system. All of them offer hope to the incarcerated and to the victims, help to those headed down the wrong path, and faith in the concepts of communication and understanding as tools to advance justice. I share their stories because they are a vital part of my own journey.

MARY PAT DONELAN

If your schedule is full and you can't possibly fit another thing into your life, I suggest you avoid Mary Pat Donelan. If you don't, you will end up volunteering your time—and possibly a good portion of your life—to the women of I–WISH.

As related in Chapter One, a phone call from Mary Pat was the beginning of FACES, a phone call for which I will forever be truly grateful. Without Mary Pat, I–WISH would not exist, the women would not have a voice, a group of lonely desperate people would still be looking for an advocate, and FACES would never have happened.

Upon earning her Masters in counseling at the University of Maryland, Mary Pat considered a career in the prison system. Officials told her she was too optimistic and cheerful to survive. "They'll beat you down," they said. She chose a career in human resources and rose to the level of Director of Human Resources at the Internal Revenue Service Office of Chief Counsel, a position she currently holds.

However, her interest in prison affairs never waned. In 1993 The Prison Ministry Coordinator for her church held an "Information Night." She was soliciting volunteers for local prisons citing the Bible's "Final Exam."[17] Despite Mary Pat's cheerful nature, her work in the penal system began.

In the years that followed Mary Pat learned most of the people in the prison were "good people who had made bad mistakes. My heart softened and I wanted to do more." She joined CURE (Citizens United for the Rehabilitation of Errants)—an international organization dedicated to reducing crime through reform of the criminal justice system, especially prison reform—eventually becoming vice president. In that role she received twenty to thirty letters a month from inmates across Maryland.

In 2007 she went to a Social Ministry retreat. The Prison Ministry Coordinator thanked everyone for their service, but talked about how much more help was needed. Upon returning home, she found the letter from Daphne (Chapter Nine).

According to Daphne, many programs were available for people who would be released, but few opportunities for lifers. Enrollment in the programs was limited and often closed to lifers because of budget restraints. Daphne asked for help in three specific areas:

1. *Self–development:* As a trained counselor, Mary Pat knew she could help with that.

---

[17]Matthew 25: 35–45: "*…I was in prison and ye came unto me…Inasmuch as ye have done it unto one of the least of these my brethren, ye have done it unto me.*"

2. *Ways to improve life in the prison:* She felt she could help the women brainstorm ideas.

3. *Help to let people know that the offenders have changed and deserve a second chance at life:* This wouldn't be so easy. She was not a lawyer. She had no formal education in criminal justice. How could she fulfill this request?

The coincidence of Daphne's letter coming at the same time as the plea for more help from the ministry coordinator was too much for Mary Pat to resist. She met with the women and, drawn by their courage and honesty, agreed to help. I–WISH was born. The group has grown and the women adore Mary Pat because they know if she puts her mind to something, it will happen. They know she cares.

It turned out that Mary Pat's cheerful and optimistic nature was just what the women needed. They decided to hold two meetings a month. Mary Pat would conduct one of the sessions; for the other she would bring in outside speakers: lawyers, judges and advocates for judicial reform. She also introduced the women to life–enhancing subjects, such as journaling, art projects, Reiki, poetry—anything that might interest the women, stimulate their minds, and ease their life behind bars.

During the meetings, the women would tell Mary Pat about some of the problems inmates face and Mary Pat would report those problems to then–warden Brenda Shell–Eleazer (below). The warden was grateful to have the issues brought to her attention and always acted upon them. One problem: a shortage of underwear for new arrivals. From then on incoming women had underwear.

She was fulfilling Daphne's first two requests; it was time to work on the third. As related in Chapter One, the women decided to launch a reach–out program to warn at–risk kids of the dangers of bad choices, the decision that led to the play, FACES.

According to Mary Pat, FACES helped the women and solidified I–WISH. "With each practice they became different people. It gave them an opportunity to give back to the community and the courage to dig in and talk. It helped them realize the experiences they had in common, and they grew together as a group. They found pride in themselves and in each other. They developed self–respect and received respect from others."

To Mary Pat, the production helped fulfill the third part of the original request. The audiences' reactions to the women's words showed that the spectators recognized the growth and change the women had undergone. "It was amazing to see how the audience responded. Even my husband cried, and he doesn't cry at anything." She believes FACES will help educate people and hopes the play can continue inside and outside the prison walls.

When asked what she had gotten out of I–WISH, Mary Pat's first response was, "It's fun! I thoroughly enjoy the group. It's like a series of college courses. Creating experiences for the women they haven't had before brings me joy. When the dramatist came in and encouraged them to write a poem, the women were resistant. But they did it, and the results were amazing."

Mary Pat looks on the women as family; the younger ones as her children. She is thrilled for them when good things happen and grieves with them when things go bad. "Working with the women makes me appreciate life. I go into the prison with problems. When I come out my problems don't seem so bad."

Mary Pat's work with the women has made her realize just how broken our judicial system is and she is passionate about the changes that must be made. "Discovering the injustices and inequities is like peeling an onion. We must make changes. We don't have to settle for an unjust system. We are bigger than that."

SUSAN EBERHARD

For the second formal meeting of I–WISH Mary Pat invited Dr. Ed Sabin (Chapter Fifteen) to come to the prison and introduce the women to the Alternative to Violence Project (AVP). Susan Eberhard, who had been facilitating AVP groups in prisons for three years, accompanied him. Like Mary Pat, Susan was drawn to the women and asked Mary Pat if she could come back for another visit. Of course, when Mary Pat is involved, there is no such thing as just "another visit." Susan became the co-sponsor of I–WISH.

Susan has an interesting history. She entered a convent immediately following high school and was educated in the Catholic system. She earned a Bachelor's degree from Marymount University in New York and a Master's in History from Duquesne University in Pennsylvania. She took her vows as a sister in the Sacred Heart of Mary Order, joining a community of strong women dedicated to education and social service. She taught school in the United States and spent five years teaching in Colombia, South America.

After seventeen years she felt the need to grow. She left the sisterhood and moved to New York where she taught history and served as a school administrator. A year later, she moved to Washington, D.C. Her boyfriend at the time introduced her to "someone who can get you a job." That someone turned out to be a man named John. John now tells people, "I couldn't get her a job, so I married her." But Susan did get a job and she worked with Blue Cross and then Health and Human Services until her retirement.

Working with prison inmates has been a joy for Susan. "I've met so many amazing people. I've learned how many extraordinary people there are in the world—such diversity and richness. The people I've met have improved my life."

She cares deeply for the women of I–WISH and admires how they stand up to their struggles: "They are so strong. They get battered down, they take time to breathe, and then go at it again." Susan tells everyone about Krista and her three–year "hit." (Chapter Nine) "The way Krista reacted to the setback was just incredible! Such strength! Such resilience!" she brags to everyone she meets.

Susan is as big a fan of the performers in FACES as Mary Pat is. She especially enjoyed the in–house performance the women gave for their fellow inmates—short–termers who would eventually be released. She witnessed the drama before the performance—how nervous the women were about baring their souls in front of people who could use what they learned to make the actors' lives miserable. When the audience responded so well to the women and Susan saw how touched they were, she could only cry. "It was beautiful," she said. "They cried. They saw themselves. The women made such a difference in their lives. I'm sure they saved some of them. It was a gift. They won't be back."

It may sound contradictory, but gentle Susan is our cheerleader. She is a true lady, but she doesn't even flinch when I sometimes let out an oath reminiscent of my Brooklyn days. When things go wrong, as they often do, she encourages Mary Pat and calms me down.

She often attended rehearsals. Sometimes, during the rehearsal process, the divas would really get to me and I would be ready to blow. Susan's soft hand on my shoulder would help me compose myself and start over.

Except once. One day the divas were in particularly nasty form. They had pushed every button I had and then some. I got mad and threatened to leave if they didn't straighten up. Susan immediately appeared at my side. She threw a comforting arm around my shoulders. "Take it easy," she whispered. "They have tough lives." I settled down and went on with rehearsal.

On that day one of our line coaches didn't show up. I asked Susan to fill in. Being responsible for every cue in the show is not as easy as it sounds. You can't take your eyes off the script; a lapse in attention, a momentary distraction can make you lose your place. The process was new to Susan and she missed a couple of cues. I didn't know it at the time, but the divas were all over her—sighing and rolling their eyes. No surprise they were the ones it bothered the most: it's always the divas and divos who never learn their lines.

After rehearsal Susan came to me: red face, tight lips. Gentle, sweet Susan was furious. She told me what had happened. "I understand now," she said. Sometimes divas can even try the patience of a former nun.

The women of I–WISH consider Mary Pat, Susan, and me their own private "Golden Girls." Mary Pat is the dynamo; Susan is the elegant presence; I am the clown. That the women accepted us into their lives is an honor we will always treasure.

BRENDA SHELL–ELEAZER

Brenda Shell–Eleazer was the warden of the prison during the development and production of FACES. It was Ms. Shell–Eleazer who first allowed the creation of I–WISH as a group designed to help lifers contend with their years of incarceration and embark on a journey of self–help and self–growth. She knew lifers were often restricted from prison programs because of funding criteria and was glad to give the women a chance to express themselves and have their voices heard. Without her forward–thinking permission and support, the women's efforts to reach out to at–risk young people would have been ignored.

Ms. Shell–Eleazer has worked in the prison system for over twenty years. She has introduced countless programs designed to help women reenter the world and make life more humane while they are behind bars. She has the ability to walk the fine line between caring and firmness. She can be tough, but her charges always know she is fair and genuinely concerned about their lives.

Ms. Shell–Eleazer is now the warden of a maximum–security detention center in Annapolis, Maryland. I interviewed her in her prison office on May 22, 2012. Our talk centered on the bias against women in the criminal justice system.

According to Ms. Shell–Eleazer, the present bias against women in the justice system dates back to the 1980s. Before then, women were looked on as nurturers who were vital to their children's lives. They often received a slap on the wrist and were permitted to continue their roles as mothers.

Then came the push for gender equality and the backlash philosophy of: "equal rights = equal accountability." Brenda saw the rise of what became the prevailing stance: "Women in trouble are not able to be reformed."

Sentences became tougher, with no consideration for the children involved. The new policies had an impact on the children and on the community and precipitated "a cycle of crime." Children, often already lacking a father, were shipped off to relatives or incorporated into the foster system, many times with disastrous results.

Then came the "Tough on Crime" policies and the "War on Drugs," which particularly focused on crack cocaine in the inner cities. "Women were involved with men in the trade and got caught in the web," Ms. Shell–Eleazer told me. "Often, the women had no link in the drug trafficking, but were considered guilty simply because of their association with the men. The men had useful information and were able to plea bargain for lighter sentences. The women had no such information and often received harsher—and longer— sentences. Since the 1980s the female prison population has tripled."

We discussed other factors that related to women. Ms. Shell–Eleazer touched upon the misapplication of the Felony Murder Law (Chapter Fourteen): The stature "does not allow looking into cases on individual bases," or require a "need to show evidence of the knowledge of the crime." Ms. Shell– Eleazer cited Talia's case (Chapter Nine) in which the fourteen–year–old's involvement with a robbery/murder netted her a life sentence, while her co–defendant, who actually pulled the trigger, received a lighter sentence in return for information about his cohorts in the criminal world.

Ms. Shell–Eleazer has strong feelings about mandatory minimum sentences that don't allow a judge's discretion following a conviction. "While some believe mandatory minimum sentences are keeping serious offenders off our streets longer [and] keeping our communities safer, the result is the sentencing of many nonviolent drug offenders to unjustly harsh prison terms where they crowd prisons already filled above capacity."

I can only hope more people of Ms. Shell–Eleazer's intelligence, integrity, and compassion join the effort to reduce our crime statistics. She is an amazing woman and I feel privileged to call her my friend.

MERLE HELEN MORROW

The one question I am most often asked when I advocate for these women is: "What if it were your mother/father/husband/son/daughter/friend she killed? How would you feel then?"

I have to answer, "I don't know."

One person who can answer that question is Merle Helen Morrow, a retired lawyer who, for three years, taught a GED class for men incarcerated in a maximum–security prison. In her book, *SO AM I: What Teaching in a Prison Taught Me,* she eloquently describes her involvement with the men she taught. Just as with my experience with the women, she went into the prison to teach convicted felons and came out having made dear friends. She keeps in contact with her former students through letters and attendance at graduations and other special events. When her book came out she was banned from that institution, but she continues to volunteer her services at other prisons throughout Maryland.

Two years after she left that prison, Ms. Merle's son, Carlos, was shot and killed in a road–rage incident. He left behind six–year–old twin boys and the basketball and baseball teams he coached. It was not just his parents, wife, and children who were in mourning; it was an entire community.

A fundamentalist Christian, Carlos loved Ms. Morrow and tolerated her beliefs, but couldn't always accept her prison activities. He had strong feelings about what he saw as justice and morally correct behavior. Nonetheless, when Ms. Morrow related a story about one of her students, this strict conservative man cried.

When Carlos was murdered, Ms. Morrow held fast to her philosophy of compassion:

> When I moved outside my grief enough to think,
> I knew I desperately wanted the killer to be caught
> and taken off the streets, but I also wanted the
> killer to have the programs and help necessary to
> bring him from where he (or she) was to a place
> where, if he returned to society, he'd never, ever
> do to another family what he'd done to ours.
> None of that impacted my feeling toward the men
> I met at the prison.

The shooter was never caught. Ms. Morrow wants that person apprehended, but she wants to see him/her treated justly. "To do otherwise would dishonor my son's name." She agreed to talk with me because, "Carlos would not have wanted to see a person unjustly punished in his name, so I see my discussing the issue as a way to honor his memory."

Ms. Morrow now travels extensively in her effort to spread the word of prevention and redemption through education. Sometimes she is greeted with enthusiasm, other times with polite acceptance and a blasé response.

At one meeting she asked a group of 150 women to sign a congratulatory card for a group of youth offenders who were graduating from the Youth Challenge Program, a rigorous educational course designed and taught by maximum-security inmates who themselves go through a lengthy training period. The program sends a message to the outside world that the participants are striving to change their lives. It was a huge accomplishment for the graduates and for their instructors. Out of the 150 women, only twenty-six bothered to sign. Ms. Morrow felt discouraged, but knew, "inmates have to have faith that a seed is planted" and the word will spread.

Ms. Morrow believes the public's inability to see criminals as people capable of redemption and change is detrimental not only to the offenders, but also to society. In order for this attitude to change, she says, we need to be involved. "We need to volunteer our experience and get into the prisons and interact with the inmates. We must pierce the closed universe that is prison in more ways than the bars and razor wire. More people need to see who the people are and hear each individual story."

According to Ms. Morrow, we are dismissing what could be a valuable resource in our fight to save our children. In a survey of prisoners, the men listed their priorities as job skills, job readiness, and education. Every man said he wanted to work with at–risk kids—tell young men about the multiple life–destroying side effects of substance abuse. Most of Ms. Morrow's students were strung out on drugs or alcohol when they committed their crimes, "…not an excuse, but a causative factor."

Ms. Morrow believes these are the people to whom our children will listen. "As mentors, they are the ones most likely to relate to the kids and get them to turn their lives around. The men are eager to learn and they want to pass their newfound passion for education on to the people who need it the most."

What a waste of a promising resource.

ARTHUR and RITA TATE

Arthur and Rita Tate's son, Brian, is a prime example of the devastation Governor Glendening's 1995 proclamation "Life Means Life" (Chapter Fourteen) visited upon people caught up in the ensuing chaos in the judiciary system.

According to Mr. Tate, Brian was a good kid: "the kind of son everyone would want to have." He was a sophomore in high school with a B average. He was the quarterback for his school's football team and an assistant coach for a Little

League football team. His record was clean; he had never had a run–in with the law.

However, adolescent rebellion set in and Brian began to exhibit behavioral and emotional problems. Everything came to a head when, on February 16, 1992, he ambushed a nineteen–year–old romantic rival and stabbed him to death. Brian was sixteen years old.

The family found themselves thrown into a legal quagmire. They spent their days "agonizing over the horrible reality of the situation. We are trying to salvage our lives. …We don't know where we are heading. It's the uncertainty of it all." "My heart goes out to [the victim's mother] and her family," Mr. Tate told a reporter, "but what happened could never change …. How do you make your lives normal again?"[18]

The state refused to try Brian in juvenile court and, because he had made threats to the victim, he was charged with first–degree murder. To make matters worse, the entire town turned on the family. They were ostracized, and bumpers stickers reading, "Brian Tate Should Get the Death Penalty" appeared on cars.

On the advice of counsel they did not go to trial. The attorney felt that Brian's rebellious nature would be detrimental to his case. They made a plea deal: Brian would plead guilty and accept a sentence of Life with the Possibility of Parole with a promise from the state he would be eligible for parole in fifteen years.

In 1992 such a deal was common practice. But then came 1995, and the Rodney Stokes incident and Governor Glendening's "Life Means Life" proclamation (Chapter Fourteen). Brian now faced the rest of his life behind bars.

In the twenty–two years Brian has been in prison he has made remarkable progress. He took GED classes and was

---

[18]"Stunned Families Try To Make Sense Of Teen Slaying" by Kris Antonelli and Arthur Hirsch. Baltimore Sun. March 01, 1992.

graduated as valedictorian, with the highest grades ever earned in the prison's course. He went on to become a teacher's aide.

He took more classes: mechanical shop, plumbing, welding, and information technology (IT). He enrolled in a correspondence course through Penn State University. He taught himself to speak Italian and to play the guitar. He also taught himself to paint and became an accomplished artist. He donates his paintings and organizes walk–a–thons to raise money for charities.

Brian has held numerous positions of responsibility in the prison. He worked in the prison laundry room and as a library aide, became an activist in the prison, and served as a member of the Residential Outreach Committee. He took on the job of prison photographer and he worked as a locksmith's assistant. Throughout the years he has been drug and infraction free.

He sought help to improve himself. He had six years of intense treatment in the prison supplemented by a private psychiatrist his parents hired. The psychiatrist did extensive testing and evaluation and declared Brian of little or no danger to society.

According to Mr. Tate, the state government won't even look at Brian's accomplishments. "Every governor since 1995 has completely ignored the intent of a Life with the Possibility of Parole sentence. They have usurped the authority of the Parole Commission and turned [the process] into a political football." Mr. Tate believes State Attorneys are only interested in winning cases and that the governors refuse to grant lifers parole because they are afraid it will cost them votes.

Brian's parents have not given up. Every time I go to Annapolis to testify on a Bill they are there, pleading for their son and for others who are in the same predicament. At this time, they are preparing for yet another appeal.

According to Ms. Tate, "When the state makes a deal they should honor it. I want him to have a second chance. He was sixteen. And it's wrong. Just wrong."[19]

GINGER DUKE–BEALES

We met at the Double–T Diner, an establishment iconic to Baltimore—Ms. Duke–Beales's choice. It was a beautiful late spring day, so I waited outside. A bus pulled up, a ramp lowered, and the biggest motorized wheelchair I had ever seen rolled onto the sidewalk. The tall dark women seated in the chair had the carriage of a queen. I stood, and she waved to me. "You must be Betty. Hi. I'm Ginger."

I walked, she rolled, into the diner where shouts of "Ginger baby! Good to see you!" filled the air, followed by multiple hugs and cheek–kisses. It took us ten minutes to make our way to the table waiting for us—a table reserved especially for Ginger. The waitress came to take our order, but did so only after a prolonged welcoming embrace. Ginger held court as more and more people came to our table to offer homage to the royalty in their midst. She introduced me as "my friend, Betty." I got the feeling that anyone Ginger met was an instant friend.

We started with small talk. She told me about her life: her four children and fourteen grandchildren; her work as a union representative for Parking and Commuter Services; her lifelong battle of standing up for others; her triple bypass cardiac surgery; the stroke that had landed her in the wheelchair; and her abiding faith in God.

Her faith, she told me, gave her strength and peace and the ability to enjoy life and find pleasure in her friends and her work. It was her faith that got her through the grief caused by the death of her son, Harold.

---

[19] *Blocking the Exit* (documentary). Produced by Justice Policy Institute and Maryland Restorative Justice with the support of the Open Society Institute of Baltimore. Produced and directed by Anne Schwab, Creative Management Services. 2011.

Harold was 39 years old. He was working as a security officer in a bar in downtown Baltimore. One night, three patrons were drunk and creating a scene. Harold escorted them out. They returned with loaded guns. While Harold gathered the other customers and herded them to the door, one of the gunmen shot him in the back. The newspapers lauded Harold as a hero.

At the shock–trauma unit in the hospital, Ginger knew her son would be okay—until she heard her daughter whispering, "It doesn't look good."

"I couldn't pray. I could only say, Jesus, have your way." When she saw her daughter coming to her, holding out her hand, "I put my hands over my ears and lay on the floor."

For some reason Ginger couldn't explain, the perpetrators were also in the shock–trauma area, laughing and joking. "Why did you kill my child?" she screamed at them. Two of them, "the hardened ones" Ginger called them, wouldn't look at her.

In the months that followed, Ginger raged at her inability to retaliate. "Those boys hurt me. I wanted to kill them. I didn't care if they lived or died. I walked down the street, tears streaming down my face."

She hated the cruel things people said to her: "You have other children." "Your son is in a better place."

"I told them my son's place is here with me." She understood the comments were efforts at comfort, "But," she said, "people should just be there. Listen. I wanted to talk about my child."

At the trial Ginger wanted to make a victim's statement, but was denied the opportunity because the perpetrators made a plea deal and the trial ended. They did not receive life sentences. Ginger threatened legal action against the prosecutor, "I'm coming after you," she told him. But authorities above the individual prosecutors approve plea deals; her suit went nowhere. Nobody ever explained to her the reason for the men's reduced sentences, which further enraged Ginger: "Victims should have more say. Victims' families need an explanation. We're left confused and hurt."

She redirected her bitterness and anger by organizing a group of mothers who had lost children through violence. The group gave the women the opportunity to communicate and express their grief. This led to a series of speaking engagements at victims' rights events where she talked about her son and what she had gone through, and educated people on what to say and do in the face of tragedy. She came to the prison and spoke to the women of I–WISH about her devastation and her hurt.

She wanted dialogue with the perpetrators. "I wanted to know why. I wanted to ask them: What went through your head when you shot my son?" She met with one of the killers. He fell on the floor, crying and apologizing. "It touched my heart." She met with that boy's mother and they embraced. "Both of us have lost our child," Ginger told her.

The meeting with her son's killer—and especially with his mother— gave Ginger strength. She began to work with the Governor's Crime Committee as a Community Organizer. She mentored young people, advising them to protest in a democratic way—peaceful and legal—and to use legal resources to change the system. She worked with people returning from prison. "We need ex–offenders to help us. Their retribution is to our kids."

As she talked about her work in the community, the vibrant Ginger I had first met returned. She told me about her participation in groups designed to help inner city youth: Safe Streets, whose motto is: "Save a Youth. Save a Mother," and Safe and Sound Youth Ambassadors, a mentoring program involving people from all walks of life. She met with the mayor and spoke at Temple University and at prisons, churches, and funerals. Sometimes it broke her heart. "A little girl asked me, 'Even if I do all the right things, I can still get killed?'"

She was adamantly opposed to the death penalty. "We don't have the right to kill people. Leave it to a higher power."

She went to Annapolis to lobby against capital punishment. She didn't live to see her success.

As she talked about punishment for murderers, her latent rage resurfaced. "I can't let them take me. They already took my child. It would give them control over me. I have to do what's right for me. God has a plan. I can't interfere. My son's death was part of Satan's plan. God has a plan for murderers. Some things are worse than death.

"The murderers don't understand: there is no way to pay back. My son's murderers took my grandchildren. There should not be good time off for murderers. I don't want to see them walking down the street." She talked about her Facebook page. "I'll kill you with my pen."

Then she told me how excited she was about an upcoming event at which she was to speak and a tutoring session she had scheduled for later that day with a troubled young man who was "just adorable."

And that's the way the interview went: the caring woman, wanting to help young people and steer them away from poor choices and tragedy, versus the enraged mother grieving for her son.

Ginger died five months after our meeting. I miss her.

LEA GREEN

Lea Green and Ginger Duke–Beales are at opposite ends of the judicial system spectrum. Ms. Green's son, Corey, is serving a Life–plus–fifteen–year sentence in a Maryland maximum–security prison for the shooting death of his live–in girlfriend.

At that time, Ms. Green was working in the United States Postal System and involved in the lives of her four other children: three girls and a boy. Corey was her baby: "He was my rock."

Sitting through the trial and watching her son being dragged off to spend the rest of his life in prison turned Ms. Green's world upside down. She couldn't believe her nineteen–year–old son, a mild–mannered auto mechanic, could be capable of murder. She knew he and his girlfriend had been having problems, that the relationship had turned toxic. But murder? Impossible.

But it happened and Ms. Green was left in a world of pain. She went into a deep depression, often finding herself curled into fetal position, unable to cope with the horrendous tragedy. She finally realized, "I couldn't do it by myself."

She found a support group, *Lifers*: people who were related to prison inmates serving life sentences—mostly mothers. She talked to her co–workers about the *Lifers* group and found that some of her colleagues were in the same position: loved ones in prison. She never knew; they never talked about it. Talking about their situations helped them and her. They cried together and shared their feelings. Soon she was tired of crying; she had to do something. Her life as an advocate for people behind bars began.

The *Lifers* group brought an awareness of the cruelty of the prison system. She discovered conditions reminiscent of the nineteenth century: chain gangs, shackles, hard labor, and isolation. She heard shocking stories about some of the mistreatment inmates suffered—beatings and rapes—stories that made her wonder: "How can one human treat another human like that?"

According to Ms. Green, many of the private penal institutions have become businesses; keeping people in jail has become a profitable enterprise. Commissaries charge outrageous prices, as does the telephone system. Prison kitchens are expected to turn a profit. Prison factory labor is cheap and profits are lucrative for the manufacturers.

She decided to go to Annapolis. She wanted to be a part of prison reform and she wanted to "put a face on the pain and misery the perpetrators' families suffer. We all have the same pain. Pain is universal. Everyone feels the same when their child is in trouble." And she wanted to find peace and help others to do so as well.

She set out to be a "game changer." She wanted officials in the system "to abandon their holier–than–thou judgmental attitudes and stop making the perpetrators' families feel less important because they have less education or are the mothers of murderers." And she wanted them "to stop driving these people away as if they had no pain."

She tried to make officials understand what it was like to have a loved one in jail. "Don't tell me I'm mourning in the wrong way. It is a living nightmare every day. What is happening to my child? There is no closure."

She wanted politicians to understand. "We [the perpetrators' families] are their constituents, too." She felt the politicos had little respect for them or for their predicaments. "When we testified, they talked among themselves." One court official waved them off with uncaring sentiments: "The correctional officers are doing what they're supposed to be doing: taking care of prisoners."

"That's not the right attitude," Ms. Green told him. "We need to make our prisons safer."

She feels what is missing from the equation is humane reasoning. "People need to understand we are all in this together." One of her biggest goals is to get the families of the victims and the perpetrators together. She believes it would be a powerful group and that it would be healthy for both sides to "come together, communicate, break down walls, make peace, and develop common goals."

Ms. Green now serves as president of the Maryland chapter of CURE. She attends meetings with families of both victims and offenders and explains her misery as the mother of a lifer. She tries to "connect the dots" in a healing process. It is difficult work. One perpetrator's mother, unable to talk about her son's crime, asked Ms. Green, "How is it possible for you?" Ms. Green could only shrug and say, "I have to."

Through CURE, Lea lobbies for more inclusion of perpetrators' families. She attended the Governor's Task Force on Violence symposium where the families weren't even mentioned. "We have to be part of the solution," she told them. "All of these boys are my sons." She talked about the violence in prisons and suggested getting the families involved would help decrease that violence. With like–minded people, she helped develop an agenda that included site visits for officials, an investigation into mental illness in the prisons, and the need for medication. She believes the glass ceiling is cracking and will lead to healing for all.

Ms. Green attends I–WISH meetings and keeps in contact with many of the women. She is a supporter of W.O.W. (Women of Wisdom), a prison organization that offers support for all inmates.

She wants to put a face on both victims and perpetrators. "People don't realize that two families are devastated."

LISA SPICKNALL

I have spent the last six years working with lifers. I have heard about their horrendous lives and read about their crimes. I was married to a psychiatrist who worked with disturbed prison inmates and brought their stories home. I have been in theater all my life, both as an actress and a director in dark productions. I've studied Shakespeare's tragedies. I thought I was shockproof.

Nothing prepared me for Lisa Spicknall's story.

The interview started the way all the others did. I asked Ms. Spicknall about her family: husband, two boys, nine and eleven, and her work: program coordinator for MADD (Mothers Against Drunk Driving). In that position she assists victims and their families: accompanies them to court, guides them through paper work, offers suggestions for their victims' rights' statements, and arranges for help with household necessities.

She told me she is proud of her work with MADD and the successes of that organization: lowering the drinking age; reducing the legal limit for alcohol intake from .10 to .08; lobbying for tougher penalties for drunk driving; and encouraging the use of designated drivers, especially when kids are behind the wheel.

Then I asked what had happened to her. In a calm voice she said, "My ex–husband shot and killed my three–year–old daughter, Destiny and my two–year–old son, Richie."

For at least a full minute I was unable to speak.

After years of physical and emotional abuse, Ms. Spicknall left her husband and filed a restraining order. Several weeks later, Mr. Spicknall collected the children for a weekend at the beach. Ms. Spicknall was not concerned about the children's safety; her husband's violence had always been directed at her.

Two weeks before Mr. Spicknall had filed an application at a Prince George's County pawnshop to purchase a handgun. Even though it is illegal to purchase a gun when under a restraining order, because of a clerical error the request was approved. On September 8, 1999 Mr. Spicknall picked up the children, put them in their car seats, drove to a construction site, and shot them. Richie died almost immediately; Destiny lived for thirty–six hours, unconscious but calling for her mommy.

Devastated by the death of her children and her ex–husband's actions, Ms. Spicknall could only think of suicide. A police detective told her Mr. Spicknall might evade conviction without her testimony—a lie for which Ms. Spicknall remains grateful. Mr. Spicknall was convicted and sentenced to life in prison where, seven years later, he was strangled to death.

Following her children's murder, Ms. Spicknall joined a support group for people who had lost loved ones through violence. Impressed by her demeanor and courage, the director recruited her as a group leader.

Her experience with victims and their families led to working with offenders. It was difficult at first. The fact they were rapists and murderers was always in the back of her mind. But as she got to know them, as they became friends, she began to realize most of them were not the same people they were at the time of their crimes. One of the older men had been in prison since the age of fifteen.

Many of the inmates wanted to atone for their crimes in some way; they just didn't know how to go about it. Ms. Spicknall began to work with the Inmates Works Program, a group staffed by Restorative Justice practitioners (Chapter Fifteen) and Victims' Services personnel and volunteers. The program offered ways in which offenders could benefit the community.

- They walked to earn money for victims' services.
- They cleaned a veterans' cemetery.
- They cared for retired racehorses.
- They helped to replenish an oyster bay
- They rebuilt a Skipjack for a town that didn't have the manpower or the money to work on the historical boat.
- They built handicap ramps on sidewalks.
- They made bricks for the city.
- They participated in a program that trained service dogs.

The men came up with their own ideas:

- They made baby bibs for homeless shelters.
- They made baby blankets in which police could wrap infants when all evidence must remain at a crime scene.
- They made teddy bears for police to give to frightened children.
- They made handbags and large "escape bags" for abused women on the run.

These programs helped the men as well. They mastered new skills, learned responsibility, and demonstrated good behavior. It gave them a stake in the community.

Ms. Spicknall also participates in the VOICES program (Victim Offender Impact Crime Education), a program that allows offenders to see how their crimes impacted on their victims. It sensitizes them to the results of their actions: children, robbed of their innocence and security, who wet their beds or could no longer sleep in their own rooms.

She found the programs did more than help victims. Many institutions are now allowing the Mediation and Conflict Resolution Center (Chapter Fifteen) to bring offenders' families and victims together in "Family Mediation." The process builds bridges between the two sides, putting a face on both, and helps returning citizens with their reentry into society.

Ms. Spicknall feels all offences must be handled on a case–by–case basis. Forgiveness is possible, she says, but only if the individual "shows change and expresses true and meaningful remorse for his or her crime." While it is true the offenders made bad choices, "We all make choices," Ms. Spicknall said, "but most of the choices we make don't affect the rest of our lives."

Ms. Spicknall knows she will never fully find peace; she still cries when she drives past the cemetery where Destiny and Richie are buried. She has since remarried. Her sons, Zachary and Liam, wonder about their sister and brother and wish they could have known them. "My life will never be the same. I am living a 'New Normal.' But I can either let the tragedy consume me or I can move forward. I choose to move forward."

Ms. Spicknall's courage is an inspiration to everyone she meets. She speaks to victims' groups about her loss and encourages others to move forward as well. Her bravery gives others hope. She has turned an unspeakable tragedy into a lesson in valor.

WALTER LOMAX

Walter Lomax is one of the most remarkable people I have ever met. In 1969, at age twenty, he was sentenced to life in prison for a robbery and murder he did not commit. He was functionally illiterate and facing life in an institution in which there were no structured educational programs or opportunities for growth and self–improvement. When education programs were brought into place, he earned his

GED and AA degrees.

In 1990 Centurion Ministries of New Jersey investigated the crime and, convinced of Mr. Lomax's innocence, took on his case. Sixteen years later—after thirty–nine years of incarceration for a crime of which he was innocent—they finally secured his release. "Without them I would still be in prison," Mr. Lomax told me.

His release, however, did not clear his record. It wasn't until April 2, 2014—forty–five years after his arrest—that Mr. Lomax prevailed on a Petition of Actual Innocence in a Baltimore court and cleared of all charges. "The vindication was long in coming," Mr. Lomax said. "But I lived up to my motto, 'Never give in. Never give up.' It was a wonderful experience, almost a half–century of my life entangled in the criminal justice system. I was finally free of the horrible tragedy."

After nearly forty years in jail for a crime he did not commit, you would think he would come out an embittered hardened criminal, ready to take revenge on the world. Instead, he is a consummate gentleman who has dedicated his life to helping those he left behind. His book: *Mandela Conquers the Cut: Essays from prison,* is a collection of writings from his seven years as editor of the prison magazine, *The Conqueror*. The essays and editorials in Mr. Lomax's book "reflect the culture, mindset, and pulse" of the Maryland House of Corrections (also known as The Cut), a notorious prison that was closed in 2007.[20]

For the first twenty–four years, from 1969 to 1993, Mr. Lomax didn't really know his fellow inmates; in fact he had little interest in learning about them. He worked his way up the arduous ladder of inmate promotion: maximum–security to medium–security to minimum–security, to Work Release to Family Release. Each step required extensive psychological testing and each step was years apart. Mr. Lomax had been on

---

[20]"In Surprise Move, Md. Closes Jessup Prison, Transfers Inmates." By Rosalind S. Helderman. *The Washington Post*. March 19, 2007.

both Work Release and Home release for five years, working at a warehouse and enjoying once a month weekends with his family, when he got caught up in the 1993 Rodney Stokes incident described in Chapter Fourteen. The police came to his workplace, put him in handcuffs and shackles, and took him back to prison.

Mr. Lomax began to get to know his fellow prisoners and listen to their stories. "I saw warehoused people with overwhelming accomplishments. I paid more attention to the men as individuals. I began to realize what was being done to them—saw the wrongs. Saw the change in the men. I began to realize the men released were not threats—they were doing well."

In 1996, an inmate named Gerald Fuller submitted a Writ of Habeas Corpus,[21] claiming the "Life Means Life" policy (Chapter Fourteen) violated his plea agreement. The court denied the petition because technically Mr. Fuller was not eligible for parole.

However, this gave Mr. Lomax the impetus to file his own petition and to encourage others to do the same. He started in the Circuit Court—denied. On to the Court of Special Appeals—denied. Then to the Court of Appeals, where in 1999 his petition (Lomax v. State) was denied for the last time. However, word had gotten out and soon Writ of Habeas Corpus petitions were flooding the Maryland courts, eventually turning into a class action suit.[22]

---

[21]Latin for "that you have the body." A writ of habeas corpus is used to bring a prisoner or other detainee (e.g. institutionalized mental patient) before the court to determine if the person's imprisonment or detention is lawful. Legal Information Institute. www.law.cornell.edu/wex/habeas_corpus.

[22]A class action is a procedural device that permits one or more plaintiffs to file and prosecute a lawsuit on behalf of a larger group, or "class". Put simply, the device allows courts to manage lawsuits that would otherwise be unmanageable if each class member (individuals who have suffered the same wrong at the hands of the defendant) were required to be joined in the lawsuit as a named

When the prison administration discovered Mr. Lomax was the instigator behind the petitions, they transferred him to the Maryland House of Corrections in order to disrupt the process. "They thought, by sending me there, I wouldn't be able to go on. It did just the opposite: The Cut was the ideal place for me to continue my work."

This was the period when violence at The Cut was at its worst. The new policies had extinguished all hope for the prisoners. Gang activity had escalated and violence had skyrocketed. The prisoners had nothing to lose; all incentives for good behavior and self–improvement were gone. With nothing to work for the mayhem continued, unabated. The one incentive that remained, "Family Days," soon lost its glow: inmates who had earned participation through good behavior were often disappointed when the events were cancelled or postponed due to prison unrest.

In 1997, Mr. Lomax became a roving reporter for *The Conqueror;* in 1998 he became Assistant Editor, and in 1999 he took over as Editor. It was while he was working on *The Conqueror* that he asked himself, "What do we do?" His answer: "I set out to change the laws."

He persuaded the prison authorities to allow the magazine to go from quarterly to monthly and sent copies to prisons and prison officials all over the state. He wrote extensively in flowing and articulate prose. When one official met Mr. Lomax for the first time, he said, "I thought you were a little old white man," implying that an African–American inmate couldn't possibly compose such well–written material.

Under Mr. Lomax's management, the magazine expanded and included topics of all kinds: religious, medical, legal, and historical along with requests to the administration. One of the favorite columns was, "Word on the Yard," in which Mr. Lomax reported tidbits he learned from prisoners as they roamed "the yard."

---

plaintiff. Legal Information Institute. www.law.cornell.edu.

Upon his release in 2006, Mr. Lomax immediately set to work on behalf of the people he left behind. He founded the Mandela Enterprise Corporation, a conglomerate of projects with youth programs, speaking engagements, and book sales under its umbrella.

However, The Maryland Restorative Justice Initiative (MRJI) is its primary focus:

> Our mission is to advocate and promote humane and sensible criminal justice and sentencing policies for those incarcerated long term in Maryland prisons. The aims and objectives of our initiative are to advocate for policies so that individuals who have been incarcerated for many years may receive meaningful consideration for release. We believe that through actions of restoration, redemption and reconciliation, we can create long–term systemic change.[23]

I asked him why he does this work.

> I am the one person qualified to do it. I have the education. I'm able to do the research. My release gave others hope. 2012 is a different culture than one in which I was convicted. There are different conditions and different expectations in the system. My ordeal, though tragic, for the most part has ended. The real tragedy, though, is very few people cared, and those who did were powerless to do anything about it. In retrospect, if no one cared about me and my situation, and I was, and am, innocent, I know that they don't care about the men and women I left behind. I believe I can be their strongest advocate in pointing out the ills of the system, and offering solutions on how to fix it. There are many people who are

---

[23]www.mrji.org.

incarcerated that deserve a second chance.

It was Mr. Lomax and his supporters who drafted the revision to the parole system (Chapter Fourteen). The Maryland House and the Senate passed the Bill and it became law on October 1, 2011. Mr. Lomax still finds this miracle hard to believe: "That Bill was crafted by inmates and former inmates. Nowhere in the country (perhaps the world) has an idea from actual inmates affected a change in the law."

To me, Walter Lomax is the miracle.

CHAPTER FOURTEEN:
Laws and Policies

Proposed legislation to correct egregious laws

No one disputes the necessity of having offenders suffer the consequences of their crimes. Justice must be served and there are certainly people in jail who belong there. However, there are laws in our judicial system that must be re–examined. Some are the result of knee–jerk responses to "Tough on Crime" policies and the "War on Drugs" and have led to a sense of hopelessness on the part of inmates and their families.

Many of us have joined forces with Walter Lomax and The Maryland Restorative Justice Initiative (Chapter Thirteen). We go to Annapolis to testify for Bills the Initiative introduces and lobby for changes in Maryland's judicial and penal systems.

In March 2013 Maryland became the eighteenth state to repeal the death penalty.[24] We celebrated the ban on a practice we considered barbaric and a throwback to uncivilized behavior. Most western nations have abolished the death

---

[24]"Md. House of Delegates votes to repeal death penalty; bill goes to O'Malley next." By John Wagner. *The Washington Post.* March 15, 2013.

penalty and often refuse to extradite people to the United States if it is on the table. The shortage of drugs used for lethal injection is due to the fact that countries that produce those drugs often refuse to export them to the United States if execution is the intended use.

> A growing number of European and Asian companies that make the drugs used in executions are refusing on ethical grounds to distribute their drugs for use in executions, and the European Commission has imposed tight restrictions on export of certain drugs for execution, in furtherance of its position that the death penalty is cruel and inhuman. Dutch drug company Lundbeck called U.S. adoption of its epilepsy drug for the death penalty a "drastic misuse." The world's largest generic drug manufacturer explained, "Teva has shown that — like any responsible pharmaceutical company — it wishes to be in the business of saving lives, not ending them in executions."[25]

Not everyone celebrated the ruling.

JOHN KEARNEY

Mr. Kearney represents the opposition. He as an honest, intelligent man whose view of the world is different from those of us who lobbied for Maryland's ban on capital punishment. His opinion is based on extensive reading and a good deal of soul–searching.

Mr. Kearney was raised in Brooklyn, New York, the product of an Irish family. After a first– through twelfth–grade Catholic school education, he enlisted in the Air Force and was assigned to North Dakota's Minot Air force Base to

---

[25]*"How International Opposition to The Death Penalty Is Pushing State Officials Into a Corner"* by Nicole Flatow. July 12, 2013. thinkprogress.org.

serve as a security guard for B–52 bombers and Minuteman missiles.

Upon discharge, Mr. Kearney enrolled in New York University and was graduated with a degree in journalism. He went to work for the Social Security Administration, first as a Claims Representative in California and later as a supervisor in Quality Assurance in Baltimore. He went on to become Director of International Research and later the Director of the Disability Research Division.

Growing up, Mr. Kearney's own family benefitted from the Social Security system when the father died, leaving behind a wife and three children. That assistance, plus part–time work by sixteen–year–old Mr. Kearney and his eighteen–year–old brother, held the family together. He remains a "big supporter" of Social Security as it was originally intended: money for people who truly need it or are poor through no fault or their own.

However, he feels the welfare system has gone too far and agrees with President Franklin Delano Roosevelt's statement, "To dole out relief in this way is to administer a narcotic, a subtle destroyer of the human spirit."[26] Mr. Kearney believes paying women to have babies out of wedlock and the resulting fatherless children have contributed to the increase in the crime rate, and he hopes for the day when the minimum wage is raised to a point where people can earn more by working than by relying on public assistance.

In defending his stance on capital punishment, Mr. Kearney says, "Some people—rapists, murderers, human traffickers—do nothing but harm society and should, only with conclusive evidence of guilt, be removed. They have demonstrated they are unfit to live in society."

As for drug dealers: "They are the one group that might be deterred by the threat of death. They produce drugs to harm others with full knowledge of the drugs' effects. How

---

[26]Franklin D. Roosevelt State of the Union Address of 1935. http://www.albany.edu/faculty/gz580/his101/su35fdr.html.

evil must they be? Yes, they should be put to death. Maybe the threat will stop some of them from peddling their poison."

Mr. Kearney summed up his view this way:

> The issue is complicated. Everyone dies—for most people death is tortuous. Life in prison is not nice. It might be kinder in the long run to end these people's lives. By ending their lives we are doing them a favor and a favor for society.
> Lifers in prison feel they can do anything because nothing can be done to them. They have killed correctional officers and other inmates.
> My goal in life has been to make life as good as possible for as many people as possible. That's what ending the lives of these very damaged people will do.
> While the death penalty may be considered barbaric by Western elites, it is important to consider that it has been regarded as an important method in dealing with crime throughout human history, and is still considered such throughout the non–Western world.
> Let me put it this way: Would we have a better world without them? The answer is: yes.

I asked Mr. Kearney if he could do it—if he could pull the switch or administer the lethal drug.

> Yes. Because [murderers] are a danger to innocent people and always will be. They have no redeeming qualities. If something could be done to make them not want to hurt other people [it would be different]. But that's not possible. As long as they are alive they will want to hurt and kill others. They are twisted.
> In a way I feel for these people. They are sick. They didn't choose to be the way they are. [So many] had horrific childhoods [and were] abused as children. In a sense it is more compassionate to

end their lives. If we had cures for these people I wouldn't feel this way. But we don't. Maybe someday we will.

****

STATES WITH THE DEATH PENALTY (32)

Alabama	Louisiana	Pennsylvania
Arizona	Mississippi	South Carolina
Arkansas	Missouri	South Dakota
California	Montana	Tennessee
Colorado	Nebraska	Texas
Delaware	Nevada	Utah
Florida	New Hampshire	Virginia
Georgia	North Carolina	Washington
Idaho	Ohio	Wyoming
Indiana	Oklahoma	**ALSO**
Kansas	Oregon	- U.S. Government
Kentucky		- U.S. Military

STATES WITHOUT THE DEATH PENALTY (18)
(YEAR ABOLISHED IN PARENTHESES)

Alaska (1957)	Michigan (1846)	West Virginia (1965)
Connecticut** (2012)	Minnesota (1911)	Wisconsin (1853)
Hawaii (1957)	New Jersey (2007)	
Illinois (2011)	New Mexico* (2009)	**ALSO**
Iowa (1965)	New York (2007)#	District
Maine (1887)	North Dakota (1977)	of Columbia
Maryland*** (2013)	Rhode Island (1984)^	(1981)
Massachusetts (1984)	Vermont (1964)	

* In March 2009 New Mexico voted to abolish the death penalty. However, the repeal was not retroactive, leaving two people on the state's death row.

** In April 2012 Connecticut voted to abolish the death penalty. However, the repeal was not retroactive, leaving eleven people on the state's death row.

*** In May 2013 Maryland abolished the death penalty. However, the repeal was not retroactive, leaving five people on the state's death row.

^ In 1979 the Supreme Court of Rhode Island held that a statute making a death sentence mandatory for someone who killed a fellow prisoner was unconstitutional. The legislature removed the statute in 1984.

In 2004 the New York Court of Appeals held that a portion of the state's death penalty law was unconstitutional. In 2007, they ruled that their prior holding applied to the last remaining person on the state's death row. The legislature has voted down attempts to restore the statute.[27]

****

The 2013 debate over the death penalty issue tabled other efforts for MRJI. They have now resumed work on the following topics.
- The Parole System
- Juvenile Sentencing
- The Felony Murder Law
- Mandatory Sentencing

The Parole System

Whether or not to parole offenders has always been controversial. Some experts in the judicial system claim parole does nothing to reduce crime and point to the high rate of recidivism among paroled offenders. Others feel it is necessary to give people a second chance and believe with education and training they can leave prison and go on to live productive, crime–free lives. The Federal Prison System does not have a parole system, nor do fifteen states: Arizona,

---

[27]http://www.deathpenaltyinfo.org.

California, Delaware, Illinois, Indiana, Kansas, Maine, Minnesota, Mississippi, Ohio, Oregon, New Mexico, North Carolina, Virginia and Washington.

Statistics support both sides of the arguments. According to Fox Butterfield, journalist for *The New York Times*: "In California, eighty percent of parolees fail to complete parole successfully…but in New York state, only twenty to twenty–five percent of those sent to prison are parole violators, according to Katie Lapp, the state's chief criminal justice official."[28] The women of I–WISH claim no paroled female lifer has ever repeated her crime. I could find no empirical evidence to support their assertion, but they are far more up–to–date on judicial statistics than are most people in the outside world.

Beyond the "should we/shouldn't we" arguments, it is expensive for taxpayers to keep a person in jail. CURE (Citizens United for the Rehabilitation of Errants) addressed the cost factor in its 2013 letter to Maryland's legislature:

> Right now, Maryland is spending thousands of dollars to incarcerate people who have served many years in prison and who have been recommended for parole by the parole commission. It costs over $33,000 per person per year to incarcerate someone in Maryland. If you assume about half of those costs are fixed (facility costs and such), at even $16,500 per year per person it is costing Maryland $990,000 per year to incarcerate the 50 people serving life sentences that the Parole Commission recommended for parole but the current Governor has refused to approve. That's almost a million dollars per year that Maryland could spend on schools or other important services that are now being cut.

---

[28]"Eliminating Parole Boards Isn't a Cure–All, Experts Say." by Fox Butterfield. *The New York Times,* January 10, 1999.

In 1988 rumblings about release programs and parole for lifers exploded onto the political scene.

On June 6, 1986, convicted murderer Willie Horton was released on a weekend furlough from a correctional center in Massachusetts. He did not return to the prison. On April 3, 1987, in Oxon Hill, Maryland, he raped a woman and assaulted her fiancé. He was captured and sentenced to two consecutive life terms plus eighty–five years. Mr. Horton now resides in a Maryland maximum–security prison.

Unfortunately for Democratic presidential candidate Michael Dukakis, the election was held the following year. As Governor of Massachusetts, he was blamed and accused of being "soft on crime." Political commercials flooded the airwaves with images of a revolving prison door. Mr. Dukakis lost the election to George W. Bush.

Since that time, in both state and national elections, parole and any kind of release program for lifers have become political footballs. No candidate for political office wants to be accused of being "soft on crime."

Before 1993, Maryland's parole system was fairly straightforward. Sentences were meted out "With Numbers:" fifteen or twenty or twenty–five years to life or, "Without Numbers:" life without the possibility of parole.

With or without numbers was a huge difference. If a perpetrator's sentence was "With Numbers" chances were, with good behavior, he or she would be paroled after serving twenty to twenty–five years. Of course this depended on the nature of the crime and it wasn't automatic. The prisoners had to have a good record in prison. Did they follow the rules? Had they taken steps to improve themselves? Had they taken advantage of the educational programs? And, most important, did they show true remorse for their crimes and a desire to reform their ways? If all of these things proved satisfactory, they could appeal to the Parole Board after fifteen years. Most likely they wouldn't be granted parole on the first try, but perhaps a further appeal—usually three to five years later— might prove successful. For people sentenced "Without

Numbers," chances of parole ranged from remote to impossible.

Judges were aware of the system and often gave life sentences "With Numbers" to young offenders, hoping prison would turn them around, help them complete their education, and give them a second chance at a fulfilling and productive life.

In 1993 the actions of a convicted murderer turned Maryland's system upside down. Lifer Rodney Stokes, out on work release, killed his girlfriend, and then turned the weapon on himself. He was the fourth person who had walked away from the Work Release Program. One was apprehended, one raped and murdered a young woman, and one was never seen again. The entire state of Maryland was in an uproar. Then–Governor William Donald Schaefer gave an order that all lifers on work or family release be immediately returned to prison. A hundred and thirty–four people were rounded up that night and scattered into prisons throughout Maryland.

According to Walter Lomax, "These were mature men. [They were] no longer the angry young criminals they had been in the days of their crimes. They had to have developed maturity in order to be in the Work Release and Family Release Programs."

The first reaction among the men was disbelief. How could their lives change so abruptly? Still, they felt it was only a matter of time before the policy would be re–evaluated and the programs reinstated.

Then, in 1995, newly elected Governor Parris Glendening announced: "Life Means Life," an absolutism he later regretted.[29] People who had been sentenced to "life with the possibility of parole," essentially had their sentences converted to "life without the possibility of parole." Lifers who had learned skills, educated themselves, performed their jobs well on work–release programs, and who were on their

---

[29]"Glendening: 'Life means life' absolutism was wrong." by Dan Rodricks. *Baltimore Sun*. February 20, 2011.

way to a second chance were denied any hope of release for the remainder of their lives. All work release and family release programs were discontinued. According to Mr. Lomax, the pronouncement "…unearthed anger and bitterness."

The far–reaching result of this policy is overcrowded prisons, increased violence, and the loss of hope. "Inmates have no incentive to improve themselves—why bother?" Mr. Lomax told me.

In Maryland, the Governor's signature is required after the Parole Board Commission's approval of a lifer's parole. Only one other state, Oklahoma, has this ruling. (California had the ruling but rescinded it in 2012.) No Governor wanted to risk a Willie Horton incident, so appeals waited years for a signature. When I started working at the prison in 2008, Ethel and Clarinda (Chapter Nine) had both been recommended for parole, a process that takes multiple years. Their papers had been sitting on the Governor's desk for five years. Now, six years later, although Ethel was released under the Unger ruling (Chapter Nine), Clarinda remains in prison.

Mr. Lomax introduced a Bill to the Maryland legislature that would create a three–member independent, nonelective panel of judges to make the decision about the parole applications, eliminating the need for the Governor's signature and taking the issue out of the political realm. Even though a number of us testified in favor of the Bill, it died in committee.

Mr. Lomax's next Bill, requiring a signature within a hundred and eighty days, passed. However, so far Governor Martin J. O'Malley has simply rubber–stamped denials. Out of dozens of people with successful petitions—paroles recommended by the Parole Board Commission— submitted to him, only two have been released, and those two were sentence commutations, not successful parole petitions. He denied all the rest, including those of Ethel and Clarinda. After years of waiting, they were broken–hearted.

As University of Baltimore Law Professor Byron L. Warnken put it in his May 10, 2010 blog: "It is time to end the barbaric approach of sentencing someone to life with the possibility of parole, only to say, 'Ha! Ha! The law lied to you. We never planned to parole you—ever!'"[30]

Juvenile Sentencing

In June 2012 the United States Supreme Court ruled that laws requiring youths convicted of murder to be sentenced to die in prison violated the Constitution's Eighth Amendment's ban on cruel and unusual punishment.[31] However, the court did not make the ruling retroactive and left it up to the states to determine the length of sentences on a case–by–case basis. Minors no longer receive "life" sentences. Instead, they are sentenced to seventy or eighty years.

Walter Lomax and other members of the Restorative Justice Initiative (Chapter Thirteen) are leading the struggle for sensible treatment of minors in our judicial system. We all plan to back their efforts by signing petitions and testifying in Annapolis when the Bill goes before Committee.

The Felony Murder Law

The Felony Murder Law is a major target for the Restorative Justice Initiative. According to John Gramlich of the Pew Charitable Trusts: "All but four states—Hawaii, Kentucky, Michigan, and Ohio— have some version of the felony murder rule."[32]

There is some discussion as to the law's origin. Some legal scholars believe it was imported from the English parliamentary law during the eighteenth century, while others say it dates back to thirteenth–century English law. Ironically, England repealed the law in 1957, yet it remains in effect in the United States.

---

[30]professorwarnken.com.
[31]http://www.supremecourt.gov/opinions/11pdf/10–9646g2i8.pdf.
[32]"Should Murder Accomplices Face Execution?" by John Gramlich. *STATELINE The Daily News Service of the Pew Charitable Trusts.* August 13, 2008.

The felony murder doctrine states that unintended deaths that occur during the course of committing another felony are murders. The doctrine does not require intent to kill. In some cases the conviction for murder is sustained when a codefendant did the actual killing. Even if the death were accidental, all of the participants can be found guilty of felony murder, including those who did no harm, had no gun, and/or did not intend to hurt anyone.[33]

As the law is presently applied, if a death occurs during the course of a felony, anyone present and involved in the original felony, e.g. robbery or assault, is equally guilty of murder. It doesn't matter how the death occurred or whether or not it was intended. In some cases this makes sense. In other cases it is absurd. Ethel and Danielle's stories (Chapter Nine) are prime examples of the absurdity, as is a case Mr. Gramlich reports:

In Florida, for example, the case of 25–year–old Ryan Holle has served as a rallying cry for opponents of the [felony murder] rule. Holle is serving a life sentence without parole for loaning his car to a friend in 2003; along with three other men, the friend drove the car to a house where one of them murdered an 18–year–old girl.[34]

A more recent example is the Indiana case of "The Elkhart 4." In October 2012, five young men: two sixteen–year–olds, a seventeen–year–old, an eighteen–year–old, and a twenty–one–year–old, made the stupid decision to burglarize a house. It took place in the midafternoon when most people in the neighborhood were at work.

They drove up and down the street, looking for an unoccupied house. They chose one and broke in through the

---

[33]USlegal.com.
[34]Gramlich.

back door. They ignored or didn't notice a truck parked in the back and a watch and a wallet on the kitchen counter.

Unfortunately for them, the homeowner was home. He heard the noises and, fearing for his life, grabbed his gun and confronted the boys. In the ensuing panic, he shot and killed the twenty–one–year–old and wounded one of the boys.

The boys were convicted of felony murder and sentenced to forty–five to fifty–five years in prison.[35]

On the *Dr. Phil* show,[36] Dr. Phil McGraw did an excellent in–depth examination of the crime and the sentencing. No one, including the boys' mothers, disputed the fact that the boys had broken the law and should pay the consequences for that crime. The focus was on the sentencing.

One of the jury members, visibly upset at what he had to do, listed the four questions the judge posed for jury deliberation:

1. Was a felony committed?
   Answer: Yes.
2. Were all the boys involved?
   Answer: Yes
3. Did a death occur during the commission of a felony?
   Answer: Yes
4. Did the boys perceive there was imminent danger?

This was more difficult for the jurors but, with the presence of the truck and the watch and wallet, they had to answer: Yes.

Then there was the "But–For Test:"

> A test commonly used to determine actual causation. The test simply asks, "but for the existence of X, would Y have occurred?" If the answer is yes, then factor X is an actual cause of result Y.[37]

---

[35] freetheelkhart4.com/who–are–the–elkhart–4/.

[36] *Dr. Phil.* "Elkhart 4: Justice or Overkill?" Air date: January 17, 2014.

[37] Legal Information Institute Cornell University Law School

The jury had to concede that "but–for" the burglary, the death would not have occurred. According to the juror, "We swore to uphold the law so we had to set aside personal feelings. From a human point it was absolutely horrible. We held hands and said a prayer for the kids and their families. Knowing you're sending sixteen/seventeen–year–old–boys to jail for fifty–five years—tough. Painful. I'm still torn."

The prosecuting attorney declared the crime "a typical felony murder case," but allowed she thought the sentence was excessive.

Dr. Phil discussed studies showing that, under the age of twenty–five, the brain is not fully capable of foreseeing consequences and making rational decisions. He asked the audience for its opinion. All but three people felt the sentencing did not serve justice.

Dr. Phil agreed with them, calling the outcome "a sentencing that has gone crazy." He expressed hope for a second chance for the boys.

Appeals are pending in this no-parole state.

I have told many people about the Felony Murder Law. With the exception of the legal community, *no one* has ever heard of it. Some don't even believe me. They think I'm stretching the truth. More than once I've heard: "That can't be true."

But it is.

Mandatory Sentencing

Mandatory sentences are those sentences [that] a judicial officer is required to impose regardless of the circumstances of the offense. In other words, the judicial officer has no discretion to impose a higher or lower sentence depending upon the nature of the crime. Typically, people convicted of certain crimes must be punished with at least a minimum number of years in prison. Among

---

www.law.cornell.edu/wex/but–for–test.

other arguments, advocates claim that mandatory sentences will deter criminals, while opponents claim it is unfair [and] leads to prison overcrowding. Mandatory sentencing laws vary by federal and state laws.[38]

Warden Brenda Shell–Eleazar (Chapter Nine) discussed this issue with me. According to her, with mandatory sentences judges have no discretion in sentencing, cannot consider extenuating circumstances, and are not permitted to view criminal proceedings on a case–by–case basis. This has led to overcrowded prisons and, in the absence of hope, increased violence. Beyond that are the shattered families and a cycle of crime. Too often the children of those convicted, left to fend for themselves, turn to crime and join their parents in jail.

Judge Mark W. Bennett, a federal district judge in Iowa, is firmly opposed to mandatory sentencing.

> I have sentenced a staggering number of low–level drug addicts to long prison terms. This is not justice…
> If lengthy mandatory minimum sentences for nonviolent drug addicts actually worked, one might be able to rationalize them. But there is no evidence that they do. I have seen how they leave hundreds of thousands of young children parentless and thousands of aging, infirm and dying parents childless. They destroy families and mightily fuel the cycle of poverty and addiction…I am now sentencing the grown children of people I long ago sent to prison…
> Many people across the political spectrum have spoken out against the insanity of mandatory minimums. These include our past three presidents, as well as Supreme Court Justices

---

[38]USLegal.com.

William Rehnquist, whom nobody could dismiss as "soft on crime," and [Associate Justice for the Supreme Court] Anthony Kennedy, who told the American Bar Association in 2003, "I can accept neither the necessity nor the wisdom of federal mandatory minimum sentences."

This is an issue of grave national consequence.

Judge Bennett concludes his article with this challenging question:

> *Might there be a problem when the United States of America incarcerates a higher percentage of its population than any nation in the world?*[39]

---

[39]Excerpts from *"How Mandatory Minimums Forced Me to Send More Than 1,000 Nonviolent Drug Offenders to Federal Prison."* by Mark W. Bennett. *The Nation.* November 12, 2012.

CHAPTER FIFTEEN:
Hope for the Future

Advice from the women and Restorative Justice

There is an institution wherein the teachers lock their classrooms doors. If there is a window on the door they cover it. Uniformed officers pull metal gates across the hallways while classes are in session. The officers open the gates only long enough for the inhabitants to pass from classroom to classroom. There are no doors on the stalls in the restrooms and no toilet paper available; residents must ask for toilet paper before they leave the room. Custodians lock the outside doors. Metal detectors monitor every entrance.

In classes, the participants must use pencil to write in their workbooks. At the beginning of the following session, the next class spends several days erasing the entries so the books can be reused. Teachers have to beg friends for their discarded paper because supplies are limited. There aren't enough textbooks, so the students are not permitted to take the books home. There are forty to fifty people in each class.

A maximum–security prison? A school in a third–world country? No. A Baltimore City public high school. I have to wonder what the reaction to these conditions would be in a wealthy suburban high school.

Recognizing the imprisoned women as the true experts, I asked them what advice they would give to the world to keep others from following the paths they had taken. Not surprisingly, a common response was: "Do something about our schools!" Other expected responses followed: "Stay in school." "Don't take drugs."

Much of their advice centered on women and children:

• Help women break out of molds of someone else's opinions and views and regain their identity.

• Have more programs that lift women up to know their worth.

• Help our communities unite to watch and protect one another, especially the children.

• Help our children to be just that—children.

• Give women who are victims of rape and abuse places where they can find support.

• Give people a helping hand/ear so they don't turn to drugs to deal with their problems.

• Develop a crime/drug treatment program.

In FACES the women expressed their advice with eloquence:

CLARINDA If I could talk with all the parents in the world, I would tell them to remember that their actions, decisions, plans, and words don't just affect them, but all those who care about them. So they should think before they act. They just might miss a graduation or two, or three, or four, weddings, plays, games, late night talks, and growing pains.

KILEY I would tell parents that validation from them is stronger than peer pressure, that kids want to know they are seen and accepted. I would beg parents to see their children as they are, and validate their feelings and thoughts.

BLAIRE Don't rely on your friends too much. It is your parents who will stick by you when things go wrong. Those friends will disappear into their own lives.

JAYNA It's okay to get angry, but allow yourself to love anyway.

COLBY Think for yourselves. Make decisions for yourselves. Go for your dreams.

ANDIE And for goodness sake: STAY IN SCHOOL! You need your education. We know it—and you know it, too.

SHEILA Don't follow anyone else. Be a leader, not a follower.

ETHEL Don't be a sponge for negativity.

TALIA If anyone hurts you, tell someone. And if they don't believe you, tell someone else. Abuse is not your fault. Let me say that again: Abuse is not your fault.

CLARINDA I have learned to trust myself—kind of an "internal trust." You can, too. Learn to love yourself.

Kiley summed it up: "Develop a system that is able to dispense justice in a way that creates whole people, whole families and whole communities. The current system is broken. It takes the victim as well as the offender through destructive processes, leaving both broken and in need of restoration. We can do better. We must."

The one common thread in almost all the responses was: Communication. They advised parents to communicate with their kids and kids to communicate with their parents. One of the women explained it this way: "My father always said, 'I keep a roof over your head and put food in your mouth. You want me to talk to you, too?'"

But does communicating to achieve better understanding have to stop at home? Advocates of a different way answer that question with an emphatic, "No!" They want people everywhere to communicate, especially with issues that involve conflict. And that's where Restorative Justice comes in.

Suppose Jayna (Chapter Nine), the unwanted result of an accidental pregnancy and an unsuccessful abortion, had had someone in her life who listened to her? Suppose, in her formative years, her peers had treated her with respect and shown an interest in what she had to say? Could that have overcome the daily insults and accusations hurled at her every day by a mother unable to give her the love and attention she deserved?

Or, suppose Kiley (Chapter Nine) had been allowed to see she was of value to the world, that what she had to say was worth hearing? Might she have trusted herself and others to tell someone about the abuse she was suffering at the hands of her stepfather? Might she have believed in herself enough to find pride in who she was?

How about Shanna? (Chapter Nine) Could respect from others have prevented her from hitching her star to a boy and his gang? Could simple respect and a sympathetic ear have kept the tragedy from happening? Would the fifteen–year–old victim still be alive?

How about gang members? Gangs are becoming the scourge of our country. According to the FBI: "Some thirty–three thousand violent street gangs, motorcycle gangs, and prison gangs with about one point four million members are criminally active in the U.S. today."[40] Could incarcerated former gang members talk to young people and convince them they can find acceptance and respect in a group not dedicated to crime and violence?

Then there are drugs. Might Toni (Chapter Nine), high on PCP, sitting at home with her children, have listened to someone who had been in the same situation? Who better to talk to a person tempted by or addicted to a lethal drug than a recovering addict? My husband, Jerry, was a psychiatrist. He directed a drug abuse and counseling center in Lancaster, Pennsylvania. He always told people nothing was more effective in treating addiction than Alcoholics Anonymous and Narcotics Anonymous groups—recovering addicts helping those struggling with the disease.

And the kids. No street–wise kid is going to listen to a naïve, underpaid social worker or teacher who drives a twenty–year–old car.

---

[40]FBI.org.

Now we come to the sticky issue: the rapists and the murders. As Tim Johnson (below) puts it: "You can't unrape or unmurder someone." A rape victim might suffer emotional trauma for rest of his or her life. A dead person is dead. Does this condemn the perpetrator to worthlessness for the rest of his or·her life? Is there a way he or she can find redemption and go on to live a fulfilling, worthwhile life even in prison?

Consider the case of Jean Harris (Chapter Nine). She shot the doctor. He is dead. Nothing can bring him back. But Ms. Harris spent her time in prison teaching countless inmates to read and write and helping many others earn their GED. She improved the lives of her fellow inmates, contributed to society, and regained her self–respect.

A new (but centuries–old) way of dealing with trespasses against the community is coming into play more and more. It's called Restorative Justice and it is based on a way of life other cultures have practiced for years. The Maori in New Zealand live by the ideals, as do the North American Mohawk Indians. To the Mohawks it is "The way we live together most nicely."

Before I started working at the prison I had never heard of Restorative Justice. Then, even after hearing the phrase many times over, it remained a nebulous idea that really didn't hit home until I began to investigate the concept in depth for the purpose of including it in this book. What I learned has given me a sense of hope I haven't had for a long time.

Restorative Justice is the antithesis of Retributive Justice. Whereas Retributive Justice relies on a system of crime and punishment, "Restorative Justice is a process to involve, to the extent possible, those who have a stake in a specific offense and to collectively identify and address harms, needs, and obligations, in order to heal and put things as right as possible."[41] A complicated way to say: Communicate. Heal. Learn.

---

[41] *The Little Book of Restorative Justice* by Howard Zehr. Good Books. Intercourse, PA. 2002.

I was introduced to the concept by a number of people who came to the prison to talk to the women of I–WISH. The inmates live with tumultuous emotions: despair, loneliness, and depression. Add shame, remorse, and guilt to the package and you have people who lead lives devoid of hope. The speakers were not offering the women a road to release from prison. What they were offering was far more important: an opportunity for learning, healing, redemption, forgiveness and transformation and a chance to gain respect for themselves and from others.

The speakers' words and their genuine interest in the well–being and futures of the women impressed them and me. Intrigued by this fascinating new/old concept and eager to learn more about the hope it offers, I asked the practitioners if I could interview them for this book. They graciously agreed.

LAUREN ABRAMSON, PhD
Community Conferencing Center

Dr. Abramson is the founder and director of the Community Conferencing Center in Baltimore. She explained the basic reasoning behind Restorative Justice.

> Restorative Justice is a fair and inclusive way for people to deal with crime and conflict without outside interference. It is trying to do things in a fair way when harm is done. It is learning to live together.
>
> We live in a society where experts are inserted into our lives—doing things FOR us rather than encouraging us to do things ourselves. In the legal system, the chance to resolve things for ourselves has been taken away from us by the courts, even though we have the capacity to do so. Lawyers, judges and others decide they own the conflict.
>
> We need a way to reclaim the system. It is broken, overburdened, and biased by color, sex, and

> money. It doesn't give victims [or their families] a
> voice and it is too costly. It doesn't address
> relationships that have been damaged.
> The biggest thing is, we all make mistakes, but in
> our punishment–oriented society, we don't get a
> chance to learn from them. Community
> Conferencing gives people a structure to be able
> to resolve the conflict. It brings people together
> and helps them find a way to heal and learn.

Dr. Abramson grew up in Detroit, Michigan. She earned her PhD in Neuroscience and Animal Behavior from Wayne State University with a focus on the relationship between emotions and health and illness. Before the advent of her career in Community Conferencing, she was on the faculty of Johns Hopkins University, directing an on–site mental health service for Head Start staff, families, and children.

In 1994, she attended a seminar in Philadelphia presented by David Moore, the director of Transformative Justice Australia, a group pioneering in the "new" field of Restorative Justice. The seminar was a facilitator training workshop, the first of its kind in the United States. Inspired, she resolved to bring the program to inner city Baltimore. She saw conferencing "…as a way [people can] be healthier emotionally with each other versus with a therapist."

She promoted the process to leaders in criminal justice, education, and community development. Surprisingly, she didn't meet much resistance. In fact, people thought the approach made a lot of sense. The problem was getting people to change their way of doing things—especially the bureaucrats. It was difficult to persuade police to send troubled kids to the Center rather than throw them directly into the Juvenile Justice system where they would end up in court and possibly in detention.

In 1998, Dr. Abramson led a Facilitator Training Workshop in Baltimore with the support of the Governor's Office of Crime Control and Prevention (GOCCP). A grant from that office, along with another from the Maryland

Judiciary, enabled her to begin the program. She founded the Center in order to centralize the information, have quality assurance, and provide a place where people in the community could send referrals and arrange for meetings in the various neighborhoods.

Dr. Abramson still works to spread the word. There are now Community Conferencing programs in New Orleans, Louisiana; Brooklyn, New York; and Gainesville, Florida, as well as six similar programs in Maryland. She has received requests from other cities such as Los Angeles, California and Juneau, Alaska. She has a talk planned in Australia and training sessions planned nationally and internationally.

What began as a simple workshop in Philadelphia turned into a way of life for Dr. Abramson. "It has broken down assumptions I had about people. It has taught me to be more present in the moment and it has given me faith in human beings. I have grown, and if I've given others help and opportunities, I've gotten twice as much back. It is a privilege to be present when others are authentic and courageous."

For anyone who ever asks, "What can one person do?" I would suggest they spend an hour or two with Dr. Lauren Abramson.

HOW IT WORKS[42]

No crime exists in a vacuum. Whereas Retributive Justice relies on a system of crime and punishment, Restorative Justice is based on the premise that conflicts are opportunities for communities to learn, heal, and transform, and that providing a safe forum to resolve conflicts can prevent violence.

Participants have discovered that Community Conferencing is an immediate and cost–effective response to misbehavior and crime. Conferencing helps the victim and the victim's family deal with the harm they suffered, and it helps

[42]Information and quotes from communityconferencing.org and the Center's brochure.

the offender and the offender's family deal with the effect the crime had on them.

This is not a "way out" for offenders or a way for them to escape the consequences of their actions. Rather, it is part of the philosophy that every perpetrator should take full responsibility for his or her part in a conflict and do whatever is necessary and possible to alleviate the harm caused to the victim.

The Center offers its services anywhere conflict is inevitable:

• In schools, conferencing keeps kids in school, holds them accountable, and provides a way for parents and administrators to build bridges with one another.

• For law enforcement, it gives victims an opportunity to air their grievances, and offenders the chance to account for and take responsibility for their actions.

• In prisons, it helps residents make amends for their crimes and regain respect for themselves and from others.

• For ex–offenders, it helps them adjust to their reentry into society by improving communication and restoring relationships.

• In workplaces, community conferencing has increased productivity, improved communication, and constructively addressed conflict.

• For military personnel, it helps them re–establish ties with their families, friends, and communities.

Tangentially involved people from the affected neighborhoods often attend the sessions. Even though the issue may not have directly affected them, they see their participation as taking pride in their community and promoting a safe environment for themselves and for their families. For example, in a case of graffiti the workers who cleaned up the mess were part of the circle.

It all sounds wonderful, doesn't it? Or it could sound like a bunch of goody–goodies with yet another bleeding–heart, soft–on–crime solution to nothing.

But it works.

According to Dr. Abramson, "Of the over one thousand Community Conferencing sessions held in Baltimore, over ninety percent have resulted in effective agreements in a process that costs one–tenth of what it would it cost through the juvenile justice system."

The procedure is deceptively simple:

Step One: A conflict arises in a school/neighborhood/community center. The police take the offender(s) into custody and contact the Conferencing Center.
Step Two: Facilitators at the Center call everyone affected by or involved in the incident.
Step Three: Facilitators investigate the offense and contact anyone else in the neighborhood who might be involved. Everyone is invited to sit in a circle and discuss the matter.
Step Four: At the session, the facilitator asks three questions:
  1. To all: What happened?
  2. To the victims: How were you affected?
  3. To the offenders: What can you do to repair the harm?
Everyone has a voice; anyone may speak. Sometimes this leads to a lot of shouting and high drama. The facilitators do everything they can to avoid a Jerry Springer–type confrontation.
Step Five: The participants try to come up with a written agreement to fix the issue. It is up to them; no one tells them what to do.

After a community conference, in the vast majority of cases, "…the victims feel that justice was served, and the offenders and their families gain access to much needed community–based resources."

The Center's website[43] reports comments from people involved in conferencing sessions:

---

[43] www.communityconferencing.org/.

"Excellent in terms of defusing the problem."

"A more informal way of having people communicate with each other."

"We spoke to one another and we listened to one another. That was the biggest thing."

"It allowed a lot of people to hear each other, and that's something that hasn't happened before."

CASES

Two bored young men, looking for something to do, decided to steal a car for a joy ride around town. In an attempt to evade the police they crashed the car into a fence. Both the car owner and the fence owner were furious and wanted retribution. Could the two sides get together and come up with a deal for the boys to work off their debt? Maybe this would keep them from having a criminal record that would haunt them the rest of their lives.

I was privileged to attend the community conference for this case. The facilitator, Ms. Cindy Lemons, encouraged the two young men to tell exactly what happened and what they were thinking at the time. Everyone, including the boys' families, described how they were affected by the young men's actions and the personal and financial losses they suffered. Both victims expressed concern about the boys' prospects of ending up in jail.

After extensive conversation and heartfelt apologies from the young men and their families, the group came to an agreement: the young men would get jobs and pay for the damages themselves. The participants set up a timeline with the understanding that failing to fulfill the contract would mean the case would be turned back over to the Juvenile Justice system.

Months later I called Ms. Lemons to ask how the case turned out. One of the boys got a job at a hotel, opened his first bank account, and paid his debt in full: $50 at a time. He is still employed at that job. The other boy worked at a summer job and was able to pay off half the amount; his mother helped him with the rest. The case is closed, their records wiped clean.

I congratulated Ms. Lemons on the happy outcome. "They are the ones who deserve congratulations," she said. "For me, it is a 'wow' situation. Every case I do, when I see people resolving issues simply because they were given the space to do so, all I can say is: Wow!"

A case discussed on the Center's website involved two middle school boys. On a dare, one of them touched a young girl's breasts. The school's vice principal and the victim's father had serious reservations about the conferencing process.

It struck the vice principal as a waste of time. "I was very skeptical because I thought of it as being something that was taking the place of dealing directly with [a] problem...that I felt needed to be dealt with rather severely."

"I was very angry," the father said. "I thought it was just going to be hocus–pocus, washy–washy stuff just to do for paperwork reasons."

Following the conference, there was a different set of responses.

The vice principal said, "I'm very pleased with the result. The most remarkable thing was to watch [the father's anger] work its way [down] from point ten to point zero."

The father was even more effusive with his praise. He said it was "a beautiful experience. It helped me a lot. I was carrying around a lot of anger. The meeting freed me."

Of the offenders, the father said, "It was particularly helpful to look the young men in the eye. Talking to them was therapy for me—expressing to them how angry I was. That's my baby. That's my girl."

And then the father described what the meeting had done for his daughter. "The whole thing healed her as well. She felt totally satisfied the young men were sincere in their apologies and felt she could go on at the school with them being there. She felt safe. She's fine and it's like the incident never even happened."

Another case resulted in what can only be described as a miracle. It took place in a Baltimore neighborhood. A group of middle school–age kids were playing football in the street outside people's homes. They were disruptive, destructive, and disrespectful. Neighbors yelled at them every day and the kids yelled back. Houses and cars were damaged. The aggravated neighbors, unable to do anything about the behavior, called the police, who contacted the Community Conferencing Center.

At the meeting, accusations flew:

"They're bouncing balls off my car and off the front of my house all the time. I'm really sick of it," one woman said

Mr. Don Fergus, a neighborhood resident with two smashed windows and a broken rearview mirror was especially angry. "The money to fix the damage came out of my pocket."

The kids retorted with comments to the effect of, "You don't own the street."

Finally the adults asked the kids what they wanted. The kids said they wanted to play football. They said they had to play in the street because they were afraid to go to the park by themselves.

Mr. Fergus said he would take them to the park if they would stop breaking his windows.

They reached an agreement. The kids would pay for the damages and, when they wanted to play football, they would knock on Mr. Fergus's door and he would take them to the park. Four days a week, but not on Sundays.

It is what happened after the agreement was signed that was the miracle. More neighbors volunteered. After a while, the kids got pretty good at playing football. Mr. Fergus asked them if they wanted to form a team. The kids were ecstatic and a team was born. And then a league. Somehow they found the money for real uniforms. Mr. Fergus and his players became front–page news on Baltimore's *City Paper.*

It didn't stop there. The kids learned discipline. They knew if they misbehaved they would suffer Mr. Fergus's penalties: doing push–ups and running laps. And he would know if they strayed. He's right there in the community.

Parents pushed their kids to go to school every day and bring home good grades. If the kids didn't go to school, keep their noses clean, and do chores around the house, they would lose their team privileges.

The kids changed. The neighborhood changed. And people could sleep on Sundays.

Now more than a hundred and fifty children are involved—all because they have a caring adult in their own neighborhood. And the kids take pride in their community. "This is our neighborhood," they tell others who want to come in and make trouble.

One resident put it this way: "Community conferencing filled the gap between interpersonal conflict and crime. The incidents weren't crimes, just instances where people couldn't get along together. It helped us redefine the problems in the neighborhood and we found they were solvable by the people who live here."

Another participant summed it up: "I'd like to see the program grow. I'd like to be a spokesperson for this program. Get people involved. It can turn people's lives around."

ED SABIN, PhD
Alternatives to Violence Project (AVP)

Dr. Ed Sabin is a self–identified jack–of–all–trades. After earning a PhD in sociology and teaching for a few years, he drifted to Washington, D.C. where he lobbied for an end to hunger in America. For seven years he taught at Towson University and then went on to become a statistician at the Maryland State Department of Human Resources. Through his church, he learned about the Alternatives to Violence Project (AVP) and trained as a facilitator.

According to Dr. Sabin, AVP differs from other Restorative Justice programs because it has a spiritual side. It focuses on "transforming power," with an emphasis on "faith in human nature and the spark of goodness in every human being." It started forty years ago when, after a destructive riot at New York's Attica prison, inmates at New York's Green Haven Prison met with Quaker volunteers in an attempt to avoid what happened at Attica.

AVP is practiced at seven prisons in Maryland, including the prison where I work. The aim is for participants to experience a safe, non–violent environment, with a further goal to improve the atmosphere in the prison. According to Dr. Sabin, "the strength of AVP is that inmates and outside volunteers learn to facilitate the workshops."

The workshops accommodate a maximum of eighteen to twenty participants. The sessions are meant to be experiential; the facilitators depend upon the impact of group exercises. They do not take a leadership role; the purpose is to facilitate the process using the theory "we're all here together." The facilitators ask participants to take turns speaking and advise them to use surprise and humor to defuse conflict. They give them guidelines to follow: "No lectures. Don't talk too often or too long. Observe confidentiality." The ultimate goal is to build a community in a place where establishing a healthy community is difficult to do.

For incarcerated people, both men and women, there is danger in disclosing personal details about their families and homes. Each individual must decide how much he or she wants to share about his or her life. Many of the people who come to the group are reserved, often participating only in order to earn a certificate of completion that will look good to the parole board. But most find the three days to be a fun and relaxing break from depressing prison life.

At the beginning, most of the inmates don't know each other. They tend to be cautious and suspicious. As they play games and listen to others, trust grows. Encouraged to speak from the heart and from their experience, they talk about meaningful subjects and get to know one another in a safe environment. They find power in hearing fellow inmates and facilitators say honest and direct things.

The workshops are based on sound group dynamics utilizing:
- Group exercises
- Listening skills
- Fun and games to break the ice and play down the "macho" element

Over the course of an AVP workshop the atmosphere usually changes. Sometimes laughter fills the room. According to Dr. Sabin, it can become a "love fest."

At one Maryland prison, volunteers offer a special workshop once or twice a year on how to use AVP principles in court and parole hearings. Participants learn the importance of
- Speaking clearly
- Making eye contact
- Talking about who they were
- Talking about who they are now
- Listing positive things they are doing now
- Outlining their plans for reentry

They role–play the situation with a facilitator playing a parole board member.

New inmates may need five or six years to settle into prison life; it is a maturing process. Younger men are often incarcerated because of gang activity. Like the women, some of them are there because of misplaced loyalty to their fellow members. According to Dr. Sabin, it is interesting that the "good gang members," i.e. those who did not testify against their friends, turn out to be upstanding, respectable people.

Frequently, AVP facilitators reach out to the younger inmates in order "to help them get their heads on straight." Without preaching, they suggest values more in keeping with society and coax the young people to discover answers for themselves. They urge the young offenders to re–establish relations with their families, further their education, and stay positive when they are released—often into the same environment from which they came. They encourage those who express a desire to help others and to give back to the community.

Dr. Sabin believes AVP can be effective. "Prison officials tend to support the program and a good number of inmates who take the training continue with AVP workshops and become facilitators." They lead the three–day sessions with the use of manuals developed over the years. I–WISH members Daphne and Shanna (Chapter Nine) are AVP facilitators. Several Maryland prisons have a waiting list of inmates who want to participate in the process.

One of the goals of AVP is to reach out to kids in school—especially in training centers for delinquent youth. Dr. Sabin is convinced this different model can help divert kids from prison because, as stated on the Alternatives to Violence website, "Conflict is part of daily life…but violence doesn't have to be." [44]

KATHY ROCKEFELLER
Mediation and Conflict Resolution Center (MCRC)

Kathy Rockefeller, the product of a Methodist minister father and stay–at–home mother, identifies herself as "a recovering attorney." She was graduated from McDaniel College in Westminster, Maryland and went on to the University of Maryland at Baltimore School of Law. Upon graduation, she landed a high–paying litigation job at a prestigious law firm.

A natural debater, she was surprised when she found it difficult to work in the adversarial system. The negativity made her uncomfortable. The discomfort increased when her children arrived: "I couldn't be a bitch all day and turn into the loving mom at night."

Ms. Rockefeller spent years doing other things. She trained law firm personnel in computer software, worked in the family's auto parts store, and co–directed a large Sunday School program.

---

[44] avpusa.org.

When the youngest of her three daughters started kindergarten she took a forty–hour basic mediation course. She found it dealt with important matters and allowed her to value feelings and foster communication. Mediation "spoke her language" in a way the legal community did not. She started volunteering at the Mediation and Conflict Resolution Center at Howard Community College in Columbia, Maryland and advanced from volunteer to program coordinator to director.

At that time, there were a few agencies where the staff used techniques similar to Restorative Practices: faith–based leaders, counselors, social workers, and human resources personnel. Then–MCRC director, Dr. Charles Tracy, and others who worked in the field felt that gathering these groups together would be beneficial to the community. In 2006, with support from the Maryland Chapter of the Association for Conflict Resolution, they held a conference to promote communication among the agencies.

The successful gathering led to the founding of the Circle of Restorative Initiatives (CRI) for Maryland, a statewide organization with a mission to "connect, encourage, and support any kind of Restorative Justice that is quality." [45] With the support of many community leaders, including Ms. Rockefeller, Dr. Abramson, and Mr. Johnson (below), CRI now offers the Restorative Justice Conferences every other year. Between conferences they reach out to the public and bring groups together with an emphasis on educating people about Restorative Practices.

Ms. Rockefeller also works with youth sent to MCRC as part of a Police Juvenile Diversion Program in Howard County in an attempt to help first time offenders avoid the Juvenile Justice system. It is different from Community Conferencing: the police send the participants to MCRC and victims do not attend.

---

[45] www.CRIMaryland.org.

In order to successfully complete the program, the young people must follow a prescribed protocol. This might include writing an apology, paying restitution, performing community service, and participating in Restorative Dialogue. Police determine the final dispensation.

In a Dialogue session, two trained MCRC volunteer facilitators meet with an offender and his or her parents or guardians. They guide him or her through the Five Restorative Questions:

1. What happened?
2. What were you thinking at the time?
3. What have you been thinking about since?
4. Who was harmed or affected by your actions?
5. How can you make the situation better?

In rare instances, MCRC provides Victim/Offender Dialogue. The goal of this mediation is not forgiveness. Rather, it is a way to find some sort of peace for both sides— to find some kind of answer to the ubiquitous question "Why?" In all cases the victim must initiate the contact.

Preparation for the meeting is comprehensive, and either side can stop the process at any time. There is a chance the victim might suffer further harm. The offender may find a way to blame the victim, e.g., what the victim wore or what he or she did to cause the violence. The facilitators' responsibility is to prepare the victims for this possibility and remind them they have the power to end the process at any time.

To minimize the risk, the facilitators spend a lot of time with the victim, listening and asking important questions:

• What effects have you suffered?
• Do you "get" what may happen? (i.e., that the offender might try to blame the victim)
• If it goes perfectly, you would be able to _____?

Facilitators prepare the offenders as well. They role–play all possible victim scenarios with the offender so he or she can be emotionally prepared.

The Dialogue between the two sides is intense. In one session a victim used the chance to have her say and then ended the meeting. While it is appropriate for a victim to vent, the offender did not get the opportunity to speak or apologize. Following her abrupt departure, he told the facilitators the meeting had done nothing for him. However, at the three–month follow–up he allowed that the session had helped him realize he was not as in control of his emotions as he thought, and that he needed to work on this.

Like other practitioners in Restorative Justice, Ms. Rockefeller believes in her work and the possibility of reducing the prison population and decreasing the violence in our world.

CASE

In one particularly difficult case, a family requested a Dialogue with the young man who had raped and murdered their loved one fourteen years earlier. The former young man was now 31 years old, incarcerated at a maximum–security prison. It took a year and a half to prepare the two parties for the meeting: counseling, role–playing, and determining what each side wanted to say.

The session lasted two and a half hours. The victim's granddaughter voiced the extent of her loss; the offender apologized and tried to explain his actions: "I was an idiot, a stupid kid. I didn't know how to think."

Nothing could bring the victim back. Her family still had the burden of memories and the perpetrator will be in jail for a long, long time. But the process gave the offender the chance to face the family and express his remorse, and it gave the family some closure.

TIM JOHNSON
Restorative Practice in Schools

In September 2012, a person with the username "european_douchebag" posted a picture of a young woman with facial hair. He or she placed it under the "funny" column with the caption "I'm not sure what to conclude from this." Derogatory and insulting comments and tweets to the young woman followed,

Rather than responding in kind, the woman, Balcreet Kaur, a sophomore at Ohio State University, wrote to Mr. or Ms. European_douchebag apologizing for any confusion she may have caused and outlining the tenets of her Sikh religion. Her faith did not allow her to cut or shave her hair, she explained; to do so would be an insult to her Creator. She shared her beliefs and actually thanked the poster for giving her the opportunity to do so.

This time the comments and tweets were overwhelmingly positive. People from all over the world congratulated Ms. Kaur for her courage to stand up for her beliefs. Mr. or Ms. European_douchebag apologized for, among other things, being an asshole. Understanding spread and a relationship was born.

So what does this story have to do with Restorative Justice? According to Tim Johnson, this is what Restorative Practice is all about—communication, relationships, and understanding one another. He believes what came so naturally to Balcreet Kaur can be practiced in our Judicial System and in our schools.

Following a stint in the army and his graduation from Stony Brook University, Long Island, Mr. Johnson earned a Masters Degree in counseling from Virginia Commonwealth University. He found his studies to be unhelpful because, even then, he was not in tune with conventional methods.

He worked in prisons as a corrections officer, teacher, counselor and supervisor. The main thing he learned was: "For the most part, the system doesn't work."

He became a "Fed" in the Department of Justice where he was often reprimanded for his unorthodox manner. When he answered his telephone, rather than using the proper greeting, i.e., name and title, he would say: "This is Tim Johnson. How can I help you *right now?*" His superiors were not happy. He learned nothing in the Department of Justice was done "right now."

Upon retirement, Mr. Johnson volunteered with MCRC. He trained at the International Institute of Restorative Practice in Bethlehem, Pennsylvania and became a teacher/facilitator. He started out working with Kathy Rockefeller in victim/offender and reentry mediation, but now focuses on working with young people and establishing Restorative Practices in schools.

Restorative Practice, Mr. Johnson explains, is not a particular activity but a way of thinking. It tries to create a system of rules and expectations that will lead to a stronger community. The goal is to mend the hurt and fix the relationship between the offender and the victim. It does not focus on the crime, but on the harm done to the victim and to the community in an attempt to make things "more right." In the schools the process involves everyone affected by the offense: victim(s), offender(s), their parents, other students, teachers, and the principal.

Most schools have a detailed crime–and–punishment regimen similar to that of a prison: a certain offense = a certain punishment. Some even have a matrix of offenses— again, similar to the prison model. Only the offense is involved—not the individual(s). According to Mr. Johnson, nine thousand kids are expelled from Maryland schools each year, often creating "a school to prison pipeline."

CASES
CIRCLES

Restorative Dialogue is used in cases where there is a dispute or offense. The facilitator poses the Five Restorative Questions listed above and goes from kid to kid to help pull out their answers. The concern is not the offense, but rather who got hurt and how to fix it.

In one school where the staff had had training in Restorative Dialogue, there was a problem in a ninth–grade algebra class. While most of the teachers were on board with the Circle process, this particular math teacher was not.

The students were having difficulty understanding the subject matter. They blamed the teacher: "It sucks. You suck."

The teacher blamed the students. "You don't pay attention. You don't do your homework."

In short, the class was a mess; the students weren't learning algebra and the teacher was frustrated. No crime was involved. The problem was simply a lack of communication.

Finally the teacher asked the kids what they wanted. The response: "A Circle." The teacher reluctantly agreed. Result: The teacher listened to the students and the students listened to the teacher. They established open communication and equality. The teacher revised the curriculum and now the class works.

In the three schools that have accepted Restorative Practice, in–school detention system has undergone a radical change. Before, detention meant sitting in silence and working on assignments teachers sent in to keep the kids busy. Absolutely no talking! Facilitators suggested a Circle: "Let's talk." The kids opened up and the teachers got the opportunity to know their students one–on–one.

THE DAILY RAP

Another method of communication is also deceptively simple. It involves gathering people in a Circle of equality and getting them to speak and listen from their hearts. This may sound like group therapy, but it's not. It is people sharing interests, expressing crazy ideas, and recognizing others as human beings.

As director of my son's Center Ring Circus School's summer camp for the past two years, I have used Circles to begin and end each day. By definition, kids are selfish. They're supposed to be. They are getting to know themselves and often have trouble looking beyond their own noses. Except for a few close friends, other members of a class are just that:

"the others." Often the closest they come to identifying someone they don't know is "the one in the yellow shirt." Not very conducive to team building, especially in an environment where someone could get hurt.

Walking a tightrope is difficult; falling off a unicycle can be painful. Getting hit in the face with a plastic spinning plate hurts; getting poked with the spinning stick hurts even more. The kids have to be aware of one another and they have to look out for their fellow campers. How can this happen if all they know about a fellow camper is that he is wearing a yellow shirt? And what if, the next day, he wears a blue shirt?

So twice a day we had a Circle. We would ask a question—usually a question posed by one of the kids. Sometimes we would have combination questions when two or three kids came up with different ideas. And that's where The Daily Rap differs from group therapy. The questions are not introspective or designed to probe into any specific conflict or anyone's emotions. They are silly questions—to an outsider they might seem pointless.

- If you could invent a world, what would it be like? (Most of the new worlds involved candy.)
- What's your favorite candy? (A box of candy that's never empty was a popular answer.)
- If you could have a superpower, what would it be? (A lot of the kids wanted to fly. Some preferred invisibility.)
- If you could go back in time, where would you go? (Lots of dinosaurs involved here.)

No answer was too stupid, no random thought silly. Some kids didn't want to be involved at first, but by the end of the session everyone—even the shyest kid—even the "coolest" kid—was participating in some way.

The result: they still didn't always remember names, but the kid in the yellow shirt became, "the kid who likes dinosaurs," or "the one who likes motorcycles." The group grew closer and, by the end of the session, we were a team.

The kids loved it. Sometimes, in the rush of trying to get to all the various circus skills, I would lose track of time.

Invariably I would hear, "Hey! It's Circle Time!" And we would gather around to celebrate our new friendships and, perhaps, rehash our day with another popular question: "What's your favorite thing about circus camp?" Fabric was always mentioned, and the trapeze, and the unicycle, and juggling, but sometimes I heard a quiet voice: "The Circle."

When Mr. Johnson came to the prison to talk to the women of I–WISH he told a story:

A man died leaving behind three sons and seventeen camels. He left instructions that the oldest son was to get half the camels; the middle son was to get a third; and the youngest to get two. Mathematically there was no solution.

A wise elder solved the problem. He gave the family another camel, so the oldest got nine camels (half), the next son got six camels (one–third), and the youngest got his two camels for a total of seventeen camels. The wise elder took his camel home.

To Mr. Johnson, that is Restorative Justice: thinking outside the box in order to make things "More Right. Right Now."

CHAPTER SIXTEEN: FACES

Help the Women Spread the Word

You don't have to be perfect.
You don't have to have all the answers or always know the right thing to say.
You can climb the tallest tree if you want.
You can take chances, make miracles, or make mistakes.

The women of I–WISH and I wanted their voices heard beyond the prison walls. They wanted to reach out to at–risk young people and warn them of the consequences of bad choices. They wanted people to see they were more than the crimes they committed. I wanted people to look beyond their crimes, see their beauty, and recognize their humanity.

So, together, we created FACES and presented the production to over a thousand people. We took the play across the D.C. Beltway to The Kennedy Center for the Performing Arts, where even more people stood and applauded the women's words.

But we want more. We hope this book will carry the women's voices beyond Maryland and east, west, north, and south of Washington, D.C. Perhaps it will reach young people who need to hear—and heed—the women's advice and warnings. The more people who hear their stories and their message, the farther their voices will go to carry out their mission: *If we can help just one kid, all this work will be worth it.*

TO TEACHERS, COUNSELORS, AND MENTORS

Talk to your charges. No. Don't talk. Listen. Just listen. Hear their pain and believe them. You are able to stand between them and a lifetime of misery. You are mandated reporters. If you suspect an abusive situation, report it and let authorities deal with the problem. If the allegations are true, you will save a life.

Gather a group of young people. Ask questions. Then be quiet and listen. Have them read the women's stories out loud. For certain there will be some people in the group whose lives mirror the horrors these women suffered. They think they are alone. Let them know they're not.

If they talk about some "really cool dude" who has been in prison, have them read the chapter on prison life. When they learn about the limitations that will be imposed on them: dressing in gray every day of their lives, three rolls of toilet paper every two weeks, one pair of earrings, no e–mail, no Internet—maybe jail won't sound so "cool."

If you would like to read the play and share it with others, write to me at bettymay@mac.com. Please remind everyone within hearing that these beautiful poems, essays, and thoughts came from the minds of people we, as a society, have thrown onto the garbage heap.

Write to the women and tell them how their writings affected you and the people around you. The writers set out to make a difference, to be recognized as viable human beings who have something to offer to the world. If they succeed, let them know. Send me your letters and I will make sure your message reaches them. You will lift their depression and feed their souls.

Let the women know how people responded. Were they moved? Did they understand what the women were trying to do? More important, how did you feel about it? Did it change your views in any way? Most important: did it help the young people you were trying to reach? Did it help them think about making good choices for their lives?

One of the women told me, "If I had seen this play when I was a teenager, I probably wouldn't be here now." Maybe you can keep some teenager or young adult from taking the wrong path and ending up living his or her own version of these women's lives.

TO YOUNG PEOPLE FACING LIFE'S MOST DIFFICULT CHALLENGES

Listen to the women. Hear their words. Know you are not alone. There are people who care, people who want to help you. Reach out to them. Allow them into your life. Talk to them. Someone out there will listen.

Share the women's stories. Help people see the beauty inside the desperate woman who is serving a life sentence for a terrible crime. Add your own thoughts as well. Allow people to see you, the beauty within your soul.

"You are beautiful," the women told the young people who came to see the play. *You* are beautiful, too. You have so much to offer the world and you are not constrained by iron bars. Allow yourself to become the amazing person you were meant to be.

You don't have to be composed at all hours to be strong.
You don't have to be bad or certain to be brave.
You don't have to have all the answers or even know who you want to be.
Just take us with you in your journey,
Following your heart,
As we have just done with you.

—From the play: FACES

ABOUT THE AUTHOR

Betty May is a theatrical director, a writer, a high school teacher, a circus coach, and a clown. Her career in theater has taken her across the United States; to Europe, where she toured England, France and Switzerland with her Teens Onstage troupe; and to Central America, where she founded a company of ninety street children in a Guatemalan squatters' settlement.

She has no professional experience in the criminal justice system, nor does she have any academic credentials in the field. She went into the prison in response to a somewhat bizarre request: write a comedy about life in prison. Six years later, she is an activist in the judicial system, testifying before congressional committees and advocating for people she once knew only through horrific newspaper headlines.

Betty and her late husband, Gerald (Jerry) G. May, M.D., have five grown children: Earl, Paul, Greg, Julie, and a late addition: Chris. She lives in Columbia, Maryland with a wussy dog, a geriatric cat, and a neurotic bird.

Her work with the women of I–WISH (Incarcerated Women Inside Seeking to/for Help) has been a fulfilling and life–changing journey, and she is grateful to them for sharing their lives.

Links: bettymay@mac.com
bettymayblog@wordpress.com
Join me on Facebook
Available for Speaking Engagements and Teen Workshops

SUGGESTED READINGS

Albarus, Carmeta. ***The Making Of Lee Boyd Malvo: The D.C. Sniper.*** Columbia University Press. 2012.

Alexander, Michelle and Cornel West. ***The New Jim Crow: Mass Incarceration in the Age of Colorblindness.*** The New Press. Reprint edition. 2012.

Allison, Carol Anne Davis. ***Women Who Kill: Profiles of Female Serial Killers.*** Bushy Limited. Brighton, London. 2002.

Lomax, Walter Mandela. ***Mandela Conquers the Cut: Essays from Prison.*** BrickHouse Books, Inc. Baltimore, MD. 2008.

Morrow, Merle Helen. ***So Am I: What Teaching in a Prison Taught Me.*** Dog Ear Publishing, Indianapolis, IN. 2012.

Morse, Dan. ***The Yoga Store Murder: The Shocking True Account of the Lululemon Athletica Killing.*** Berkley. Mass Market Paperback. 2013.

Pearson, Patricia. ***When She Was Bad: Violent Women and the Myth of Innocence.*** Penguin Books. 1997.

Pollock, Joycelyn. ***Women Prison & Crime. Second Edition. Wadsworth Group.*** Belmont, CA. 2002.

Potash, Yoav. Producer and director. Video. ***Crime After Crime: The Story of Deborah Peagler.*** Life Sentence Films LLC. Virgil Films. 2012.

Solinger, Rickie, Paula C. Johnson, Martha L. Raimon, Tina Reynolds, and Ruby C. Tapia, eds. ***Interrupted Life: Experiences of Incarcerated Women in the United States.*** University of California Press. 2010.

Zehr, Howard. ***The Little Book of Restorative Justice.*** Good Books. Intercourse, PA. 2002.

INDEX

The women's names are in bold italics.
The names have been changed to protect their privacy